19. 95

UKRAINE

UKRAINE

STEVEN OTFINOSKI

☑® Facts On File, Inc.

Ukraine

Facts On File, Inc.
11 Penn Plaza
New York, NY 10001

Library of Congress Cataloging-in-Publication Data

Otfinoski, Steven.
Ukraine / Steven Otfinoski.
p. cm. — (Nations in transition)
Includes bibliographical references and index.
Summary: Gives a historical and cultural overview of the country of Ukraine with particular emphasis on changes that have occurred since the collapse of the Soviet Union.
ISBN 0-8160-3757-4
1. Ukraine—Juvenile literature. [1. Ukraine.] I. Title. II. Series.
DK508.515.O88 1999
947.7—dc21 98-7988

Facts On File books are available at special discounts when purchased in bulk quantities for businesses, associations, institutions, or sales promotions. Please call our Special Sales Department in New York at (212) 967-8800 or (800) 322-8755.

You can find Facts On File on the World Wide Web at http://www.factsonfile.com

Text design by Cathy Rincon
Cover design by Nora Wertz
Illustrations on pages 5 and 46 by Dale Williams

Printed in the United States of America

MP FOF 10 9 8 7 6 5 4 3 2

This book is printed on acid-free paper.

Contents

1

An Introduction to the Land and Its People

*O*n January 1, 1992, the monolithic Communist state of the Soviet Union ceased to exist. Most of the 15 republics that once made up this world power were suddenly free and independent states. Several of them—Ukraine, Belarus, and Moldova—had already proclaimed their independence as free republics.

While most of the former satellite countries of Eastern Europe have been able to move steadily away, however slowly, from their Soviet-dominated past toward a more democratic system, the former republics of the Soviet Union have found the transition more difficult. The satellite countries were occupied by the Soviet Union; however, the Soviet republics were actually a part of it. Historically and geographically, they are still closely bound to Russia, the governing country of the Soviet Union. Perhaps no former republic feels this bond more keenly than Ukraine.

Long before it was incorporated into the Soviet Union, Ukraine had been dominated by foreign powers—primarily Poland and Russia. Until the last century, it was called "the Ukraine," referring to a region or area, rather than a nation of people with a common purpose.

"Without a Ukrainian state, Ukrainian history was handed down as a footnote, considered no more than a provincial expression of the dominant power," writes Ukrainian-American writer Linda Hodges.

But no matter how others viewed them, the Ukrainians themselves always considered themselves a nation—one with a unique culture and civilization. Ironically, that civilization gave birth to Russian civilization, which was first centered in the legendary city of *Kyiv* [KIH-yeev],[*] Ukraine's capital city.

The glory of *Kyivan Rus* [KIH-yeev-skah ROOS], as it came to be called, eventually gave way to Muscovy, centered around the city of Moscow to the north. The center of Slavic power shifted, never to return, and the Ukraine, which means "borderland" in Russian, was a prize to be captured by one invading power after another. For the Russians it was a vast breadbasket, producing enough grain to feed much of the Russian Empire and, later, the Soviet Union. Its mines, factories, and industrial centers were equally important to those who controlled them.

Because of its importance, Ukraine was at times given a little more freedom than the other Soviet republics. Other times it was punished severely for its spirit of independence. Twice in this century, it suffered horrendous famines and world wars in which millions of its people perished.

Today Ukraine is fighting another war, one that has two fronts. On one front, it is battling the influence of Russia and its attempts to draw Ukraine back into its sphere of power. On the other, it is struggling with itself. Bitter political factionalism and corruption have weakened the new state and have all but paralyzed reform.

Too long dependent on the Soviet Union, Ukraine is finding it hard to redefine itself. Such countries as Poland, Hungary, and the Czech Republic are having an easier time in their transitions. With its floundering economy and turbulent political affairs, the Ukraine is more likely to be compared

---

[*] All spellings of place-names and people are given in Ukrainian, not Russian, as formerly known. English pronunciations by Marina Prezhdo.

The Steppes—Ukraine's Heartland

A ny American from the Great Plains might feel right at home on the expansive southern steppes of Ukraine. Both these land regions are what agriculturists call "tillable steppes": flat, treeless grasslands with rich, fertile soil.

Ukraine's steppes are part of a vast plain that stretches from southern Ukraine into central Asia. While the Asian steppes are arid and desertlike, the more temperate Ukrainian steppes are still subject to cold winters and hot summers. When a summer drought strikes, it not only withers crops but sends strong hot winds that blow away the plowed earth, causing serious soil erosion. This happened in Ukraine on a tragic scale during the famine of 1946.

The Ukrainians love their steppes with a passion that many Americans feel about the Western prairie. Just as the cowboys are associated with the prairie, so the colorful *Kozaks* [Koh-ZAH-Kih], 17th-century patriotic warriors, are inextricably linked with the steppes they once roamed.

The Kozaks are long gone, but the steppes still hold a fascination for the peasants who daily till its soil. In the words of one American travel writer, the steppes are "wide as forever, [the] horizon blotted by nothing bigger than a haystack. In eastern parts one looks in vain for a hill while standing in what seems a tranquil sea of . . . black earth."

by political analysts with a less developed country like Bulgaria, which has suffered similar setbacks on the road to democracy.

"It's a high-risk country with much high-risk potential," cites one Western investor. "When the Soviet Union disintegrated, Ukraine was expected to be the leading country. Unfortunately, it did not work out that way."

Before we examine how it *did* work out and why, let's look at the land itself and its vast resources.

Vast Steppes and Mighty Rivers

Ukraine was the second largest republic in the Soviet Union and one of the richest. Today, it is the largest nation completely located in Europe. About the size of the state of Texas, Ukraine covers slightly more than 233,000 square miles (603,470 sq km). Geographically, Ukraine is at the very center of the Eurasian landmass. It is bordered on the north by Belarus and Russia; on the east by Russia; on the west by Hungary, Slovakia, and Poland; and on the south by the Black Sea, the Sea of Azov, Romania, and Moldova, another former Soviet republic.

Similar to Poland, Ukraine is primarily a flat country of vast plains, called steppes, and plateaus. There are only two mountain ranges in the country—the Carpathian Mountains in the west and the smaller Crimean Mountains in the south. Mount *Hoverla* [Gho-VEHR-lah], the country's highest point at 6,764 feet (2,062 m), is in the Carpathians.

While Ukraine has few lakes, it is riddled with rivers and streams, more than 20,000 of them. There are four major rivers that divide the country from north to south. The largest is the *Dnipro* [Dneep-RO], the third longest river in Europe after the Volga and the Danube. It enters the country north from Belarus above Kyiv and makes its way eastward, dividing the country in two unequal halves. The Dnipro empties into the Black Sea near the city of *Mykolayev* [Mih-Koh-LAH-yeev]. Navigable three seasons out of four, it has been a major trade route for centuries.

The *Dnister* [DNEES-tehr], which is impossible to navigate, rises in the west from the Carpathians and also empties into the Black Sea. The *Donets*

This Polovtsian gravestone stands a silent witness on the vast steppes at Askaniya Nova, a nature preserve in south-central Ukraine. The Polovtsi were a nomadic people who invaded Ukraine in the 11th century. This kind of gravestone is called "Kamyana Baba," which in English literally means "Stone Woman."
(Serhiy Marchenko)

Ukraine: Physical Features

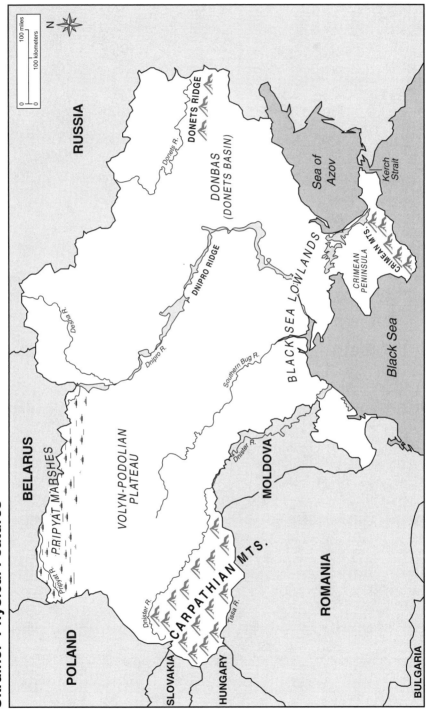

Rivers have been the lifeblood of Ukraine for centuries. Here the Pslo flows peacefully near the town of Yares'ke in east-central Ukraine. (Serhiy Marchenko)

[Doh-NYETS] runs across eastern Ukraine, while the Southern *Bug* [BOOG] is the only major river that starts and ends within Ukraine.

If the country were divided north to south into thirds, the northern third would be wooded and swampy; the central third, steppes covered with forest land; and the southern third, treeless steppes with black earth called *chernozem* [Chehr-noh-ZEM], one of the most fertile soils on earth.

Because of its size, Ukraine has a varied climate. Western Ukraine is milder in the winter than eastern Ukraine, but cooler in the summer. The climate in the far south is Mediterranean. Precipitation is much higher in the north than in the south.

A Proud People

Ukraine has a population of 52.1 million (1992 estimate). Among the former republics, only Russia has more people. Nearly three-fourths of the population are ethnic Ukrainians, forming a distinct Slavic group. There are 11 million Russians, who make up a little more than one-fifth of the population.

The remaining five percent are mostly Polish, Jewish, or Hungarian. Centuries of war and strife have caused many Ukrainians to leave their homeland in pursuit of a better life. Some 12 million Ukrainians live in other ex-Soviet republics, including Russia. Another four million live in other countries—primarily Europe, the United States, and Canada. Of the Ukrainians who remain at home, about two-thirds live in urban areas, while one-third still live in rural areas.

Wherever they live, in their country or outside it, Ukrainians are a proud people—proud of their rich heritage and culture, proud of their ability to survive invaders and catastrophes. After centuries of having their identity suppressed, they are now reveling in it. They have stripped their maps of Russian names and replaced them with Ukrainian ones. The Ukrainian language, along with Ukrainian culture, art, and literature, is taught in schools throughout the country. Ukrainian folkways and traditional customs are followed religiously by millions.

But not everyone thinks independence is the greatest thing for Ukraine. "We were strong when we were the Soviet Union," says a Russian woman living in *Donetsk* [Doh-NYETSK], an industrial center and a Russian stronghold. "But now we don't amount to anything."

This judgment may be harsh, but there is some truth to it. Promised reforms have been held back by internal dissension, corruption, and a failing economy. Transition will not be easy, but then little has been easy for the Ukrainians, as their history readily testifies.

NOTES

p. 2   "Without a Ukrainian state . . ." Linda Hodges and George Chumak, *Language and Travel Guide to Ukraine* (New York: Hippocrene Books, 1994), p. 2.
p. 3   "wide as forever . . ." Mike Edwards, "Ukraine," *National Geographic,* May 1987, p. 608.
p. 3   "It's a high-risk country . . ." *Calgary Herald,* August 14, 1996, p. D8. CD NewsBank.
p. 7   "We were strong when we . . ." Mike Edwards, "Ukraine: Running on Empty," *National Geographic,* March 1993, pp. 47–48.

2

One Land, Many Masters

(Prehistory to 1922)

*I*t is not difficult to understand why many Russians feel Ukraine should remain a part of their nation. It was here in the city-state of Kyiv that Russian civilization was first born around A.D. 800. But human history in Ukraine began long before that.

Archaeologists estimate that early people were living in the region as far back as 150,000 B.C. For thousands of years, these peoples were nomadic hunters. By about 4000 B.C., people called Trypillians had cultivated crops and were living in crude villages. Little is known of the Trypillians other than that they lived in clan groups, built rectangular log houses, and made fine pottery.

More nomadic warrior groups started to migrate into the flat steppes of present-day Ukraine by about 1000 B.C. Among the first were the Cimmerians, who entered the Crimean area of southern Ukraine. They were driven into present-day eastern Turkey by the more savage Scythians around 700 B.C. The Scythians dominated Ukraine for the next 500 years, setting up a noble ruling class.

By about A.D. 500, various Slavic tribes, wandering the land in the wake of the Scythians, settled in southern Ukraine near the Black Sea. There they were safe from the Huns of central Asia. These superb warriors began to invade the Scythians' land about A.D. 300. Into this confusing mix of quarreling Slavic tribes entered the people who would succeed in unifying them into one people: the Varangians, or as the Slavs called them, Rus. The Rus were actually Vikings, probably from Denmark, and were led by the great warrior *Rurik* [ROOH-reek]. Rurik set up his headquarters in the city of Novgorod, but his successors found a city to the south that was a more strategic center for their operation: Kyiv.

The Rise of Kyivan Rus

More than a city, Kyiv was a city-state, similar to those of ancient Greece, whose influence extended far beyond the city walls. As Russian historian V. O. Kluchevsky states, Kyivan Rus was clearly "the birthplace of Russian nationality." Most Ukrainians today prefer to call it Kyivan Rus, while contemporary Russians prefer the term Kyivan Russia, linking the Kyiv city-state directly to the Russian Empire that later grew up around the city of Moscow.

By whatever name it is known, Kyiv quickly became one of the largest powers in medieval Europe. Located on the western banks of the Dnipro River, it was a major trading center between northern Europe and the Byzantine Empire to the south. Under the seventh ruler of the Rurik dynasty, *Vladymyr* [Volo-DIH-mer] the Great (see boxed biography) the Kyiv city-state entered its "golden age." A pagan like his ancestors, Vladymyr converted to Christianity in A.D. 987. Christianity was becoming the main religion of kings and princes throughout Europe, and Vladymyr saw the religion as a way to unify all the people of his kingdom into one powerful state.

Before converting, the king sent messengers to observe both the Roman Catholic Church and the Orthodox Byzantine Church.* Less impressed by

---

* Due to differences regarding dogma and politics, the Christian church split during the 11th century.

When Vladymyr the Great converted to Christianity in A.D. 987, he gave his subjects little choice in the matter. This 19th-century engraving, shows the people of Kyiv and Novgorod being forcibly baptized en masse by Vladymyr's minions. The broken statue in the background is presumably of a pagan god. (Corbis)

Vladymyr the Great (reigned 980–1015)

Everything about Vladymyr I of Kyiv was bigger than life. Terrible tyrant, brilliant administrator, stalwart soldier—he was all these things. He began his reign as a pagan, with at least seven wives, who fiercely persecuted Christians and other religious peoples. He later converted to Christianity and spread the faith among his subjects, using the same zeal with which he had previously persecuted it.

Vladymyr's conversion may well have been more political than spiritual. After becoming a Christian, he married Anna, the sister of the Byzantine emperor Basil I, thus linking his kingdom with the greatest in the Eastern world. He strategically steered his children into marriages with the children of the kings and queens of several European powers.

Vladymyr turned Kyiv into a mighty fortress, safe from the many invaders who had plundered it regularly. Later, he transformed Kyiv into a center of culture and learning, building schools, libraries, and ornate churches.

As a soldier, he won back lands taken by the Poles to the west and defeated the Lithuanians, a threat from the north. By 1000, after 20 years of his rule, Kyivan Rus was the second largest empire in Europe, following only the Holy Roman Empire.

When Vladymyr was an old man, his son, Yaroslav, rebelled against him. After Vladymyr's death, his sons fought each other for 20 years to determine who would succeed him. Yaroslav finally emerged the victor. He proved to be a strong leader and truly his father's son. As for Vladymyr the Great, former pagan, the Ukrainian Orthodox Church made him a saint.

the rites of the Roman church, the messengers had this to say about the services they attended at the Cathedral of Hagia Sophia in Constantinople: "We knew not whether we were in heaven or on earth. For on earth there is no such splendor or such beauty, and we are at a loss to describe it."

Vladymyr was impressed by their report and chose the Orthodox Church, aligning himself with Byzantium, which became a powerful ally of Kyivan Rus for centuries to come. Vladymyr built churches, oversaw the conversion of all his subjects, forcibly if necessary, and built a state that would develop further under the rule of his son, *Yaroslav* [Ia-ros-

LAHV] the Wise (978–1054). Yaroslav promoted the arts, built towns, and created a system of laws to govern by. Under him, Kyiv's population rose to 80,000, making it as large as Paris, the biggest city in western Europe at that time.

Kyiv was far more progressive than the cities to the west. The peasantry was free and not bound to the land as under the feudal system in most European countries. Towns had democratic assemblies, or *veches* [VEH-ches], which were open to all free men, although their decisions had to be unanimous.

But even at the height of its greatness, fortunes began to shift. The flat steppes tempted still another invader from the east. These were the

Vladymyr I well deserved the title "The Great." He built Kyivan Rus into the second largest empire in Europe by the year 1000. (The New York Public Library Picture Collection)

Polovtsi [POH-lov-tsih], who were driven back by *Manomekh* [Mah-noh-MAKH], Yaroslav's grandson. The leaders who came after Manomekh were weak, and their power was divided by warring factions within the nobility. By 1169, Kyiv was seized and looted by one of its own, prince *Andrei Bogolyubsky* [Ahnd-RIY Boh-goh-LYUH-skiy], who declared himself grand prince and made the new city of Vladymyr his capital.

By then, however, Kyiv was already losing importance as a trading center. The Crusades, a series of religious wars to regain the Holy Land in the Near East, opened up new trade routes across the Mediterranean, making the route through Kyiv obsolete. The unity of Rus fell apart, and many princes and nobles went their own way. Some moved to the northeast, where in a wilderness they would establish the city of Moscow and develop a new city-state called Muscovy.

Under the Mongols and Poles

Meanwhile in the east, another invading group, led by the great Genghis Khan (1162–1227), was drawing west. The Mongols, fearless warriors on horseback, were the greatest conquerors to emerge from Asia. They also knew something about governing those they conquered. After a series of bloody conflicts, the Mongols conquered Kyiv in 1223. In victory, these fierce warriors showed no mercy. They forced the princes of Kyiv to lie on the ground and then built a wooden platform above them. When the Mongols entered the platform for a feast, the princes were literally crushed to death. Within a decade, nearly all of Kyivan Rus was under Mongol control and would remain so for two centuries.

The Mongol Empire was too far-flung to control, and the Mongols were poor administrators. When their empire began to crumble, the power vacuum they left was quickly filled by Lithuania and then a rising kingdom to the west—Poland. The Poles took over the fallen Kyivan lands, now called *Ukrainia* [Uhk-rah-YEEH-nah], or borderlands, in 1569. Although bound to the Ukrainians by ethnic background, the Poles did not deal kindly with their conquered neighbors. They seized peasants' land and created a serf system, whereby Ukrainian peasants were treated as little better than slaves and were tied for life to the land they worked. Worse still, the Poles imposed their religion, Roman Catholicism, on the devout Orthodox Ukrainians.

The Tatars, part of the Mongol invasion, attacked Kyiv in 1235, destroying every thing in their path, including the Desyatinnaya church, shown here. The Mongols ended the golden age of Kyivan Rus and ruled the country for two centuries. (Corbis-Bettmann)

Resistance against Polish rule arose among the intelligentsia, which consisted primarily of learned monks living in old established monasteries. They kept the Orthodox faith alive in the books they wrote during these dark times. But there was more active resistance, too. Bands of peasant soldiers on horseback rode through the Ukrainian frontier. The Turks called them *Kozaks,* meaning outlaws, or free men, in Turkish.

The Kozaks, or Cossacks in English, were brave and bold warriors and figures of romantic heroism, as this excerpt from an early Ukrainian poem makes clear:

> But my men of Kursk are tried warriors—
> Swaddled to the sound of trumpets,
> Lulled beneath helmets,
> Nursed from the point of the spear. . . .
> Their bows are strung, their quivers filled.
> Their swords are keen.
> Like gray wolves they plunge through the steppe,
> Seeking glory for themselves and honor for their
> prince.

The Kozaks gained their freedom by fighting for the Poles and the Muscovites against the Tatars, another invader from the east. In return for their military service, the Poles granted the Kozaks many privileges that other Ukrainians did not have. They were free to move about at will and to largely govern themselves.

Day of the Kozaks

By the 16th century, the Poles were ready to curtail the Kozaks' powers, which they saw as a threat to their empire. In response, many Kozaks revolted. They became freedom fighters not only for themselves, but for all Ukrainians who supported and admired them.

Kozak chieftains were called *hetmen* [GHET-mahn] and they were democratically elected from within each band or group. One of the most powerful hetmen was *Bohdan Khmelnytsky* [Bohg-DAHN Khmel-NITS-Kiy] (1595–1657). Khmelnytsky became a Kozak by choice, not birth. He was a member of the gentry and was persecuted by a wealthy Polish family who held a grudge against him. The family burned his home and killed one of his sons. When Khmelnytsky complained to the Polish authorities, they threw him in prison. A friend helped him escape, and he immediately joined the Kozaks. In the spring of 1648, Khmelnytsky led an uprising against the Poles. When they sent a legion of loyal Kozaks to attack Khmelnytsky, they ended up joining his cause.

The Kozaks defeated the Poles in two decisive battles and then marched with thousands of followers to the western border of Poland. Khmelnytsky entered Kyiv in triumph on Christmas Day 1649. But the struggle against Poland would not be won easily. A peace treaty that same year called for a Polish-Ukrainian Commonwealth, but it lasted only a short time before war again erupted.

The Kozaks were now powerful enough to carve out their own independent state within the Ukraine, but they were not strong enough to maintain it without constant struggle with the Poles. In 1654, Hetman Khmelnytsky made a fateful decision that would determine the destiny of his country for centuries to come. He turned to the Russians for help. In exchange for Russia's support in their fight against the Poles, the Ukrainian Kozaks took an oath of allegiance to the Russian czar. The

Bohdan Khmelnytsky was one of the great Kozak leaders of the 17th century. He defeated the Poles in 1648 and liberated Kyiv the following year. But then Khmelnytsky formed a fatal alliance with Russia that would eventually bring Ukraine under Russian dominance. (Corbis)

two powers signed the Treaty of *Peruyaslav* [Peh-reh-IAS-leev] (1654), uniting their countries.

But Russia's motives were more selfish than altruistic. It had its own designs on the rich, fertile Ukraine, which it hoped to take from Poland's grip. Following Khmelnytsky's death in 1657, Russia dropped all pretense of an "alliance." It sent a military force to the Ukraine and appointed a Russian governor to rule it. The Kozaks abruptly shifted their allegiance and joined up with their old enemy Poland to fight the Russians. The combined forces of Kozaks, Poles, and Lithuanians defeated the Russians at the Battle of Konotip in 1659.

It was, however, a temporary victory in a war the Ukrainians were destined to lose. In 1666, Poland and Russia realigned together and divided the Ukraine between them. Russia took the half that was east of the Dnipro River, and Poland took the half to the west.

Under the Heel of the Russian Empire

Throughout the 18th century, Russian power steadily increased in the Ukraine, while the power of the Kozaks steadily weakened. By 1781, the hetmanate ceased to exist. Around the same time, Poland had fallen to Russia and Austria and was itself partitioned between its neighbors. Western Ukraine, previously under Polish control, now came into Russian hands.

The Russian Empire continued to take the Ukraine's rich agricultural and industrial resources, giving little back. Russian emigrants took over the land, displacing Ukrainian families who had lived there for generations. Some peasants went to work for their new Russian landlords. Although they were allowed to worship freely in their Orthodox churches, new churches could not be built in the Ukrainian style but had to conform to Russian standards.

The Ukrainians seethed inwardly under the czar's rule. They were not alone. Other peoples within the empire, and even inside Russia itself, were unhappy with the czar's autocratic government. Russian aristocrats and other people in many parts of the empire began a secret plot to overthrow the czar. One group of revolutionaries in Kyiv were led by a former army officer *Pavel Pestal* [Pahv-LOH PES-tahl], who proposed shooting the royal family and then unifying all peoples living within the Russian state.

In December 1825, shortly after the death of Alexander I (1777–1825) and the induction of the new czar, Nicholas I (1796–1855), a group called the Decembrists rose up in St. Petersburg. The czar's loyal troops quickly quelled the revolt in that city, and its leaders were exiled or executed. Nicholas I had been seriously frightened by the attempted revolt. In response, he cracked down on dissent, imposed heavy censorship, and created a secret police force to watch over the population for any signs of discontent. The crackdown made a bad situation worse in the Ukraine, but despite the repression, or because of it, by the mid-1800s a national reawakening took place. This movement was led by Ukrainian historian *Mikhaylo Hirshesky* [Mi-HI-lo Hir-SHES-Kiy] and poet *Taras Shevchenko* [Tah-RAHS Shev-CHEN-Koh] (1814–1861), an ex-serf who was also a playwright, painter, and social critic.

In 1905, another revolution broke out in St. Petersburg. This time, Ukraine would be directly involved. A large group of demonstrators led by a priest descended on the czar's Winter Palace in St. Petersburg. They were fired on by soldiers in what would come to be called "Bloody Sunday." In the months that followed, assassinations, demonstrations, and other events erupted across the country.

In the Black Sea, sailors aboard the battleship *Potemkin* mutinied against their officers and sailed their ship to the Ukrainian seaport of Odesa [o-DEH-sah]. The people of Odesa welcomed the mutineers as heroes. News of these events reached the czar, and he immediately sent troops to the city. What followed is memorably captured in Russian filmmaker Sergei Eisenstein's classic 1925 film *Potemkin,* as Kozaks marched with bayonets drawn upon the people of Odesa. These same Kozaks would at one time have been defending these people instead of killing them.

Revolution and Independence— For a While

Another revolution was put down, but the Russian Empire was sick and dying. Nicholas II (1868–1918), successor to Alexander II, was a weak and indecisive czar, surrounded by bad advisers who urged him to keep a firm line with the people. Long-needed reforms were ignored or put off, and when World War I began, the populace felt little patriotic fervor for their country. Thousands of Russian and Ukrainian soldiers died at the front, and the war quickly became an unpopular one.

In March 1917, the Russian people had reached their limit and rebelled. Within weeks, Nicholas stepped down from power and a provisional government took control of the country. A socialist government led by Alexander Kerensky (1881–1970) proved ineffective, and the Bolsheviks, who were Communist revolutionaries, seized the government in the October Revolution of 1917. For two years, a bloody civil war was waged between the Bolsheviks and the anti-Communists who wanted to take back the country.

In Ukraine, national leaders saw the revolution as an opportunity for independence after 200 years of Russian domination. The Central Council of Ukraine met in Kyiv and declared their land a free republic. On January 22, 1918, the Ukrainian National Republic was born, naming Professor *Mykhaylo Hrushevsky* [Mih-HI-loh Ghroo-SHEV-Skiy] (1866–1934), a scholar and celebrated historian, as its first president.

When World War I ended in November 1918, the Ukrainian National Republic was officially recognized by the Western Allies, including the United States. Even the government of Bolshevik leader V. I. Lenin (1870–1924) recognized the new republic. It looked as though the dream of Ukrainian independence, lost since the days of Kyivan Rus, had at last been fulfilled.

The new national anthem, with words from a 19th-century poem, expressed the people's optimism:

> Ukraine is not yet dead, nor its glory and freedom,
> Luck will smile on us brother—Ukrainians.
> Our enemies will die, as the dew does in the sunshine,
> And we, too, brothers, we'll live happily in our land.

But their happiness would be short-lived. A free Ukraine was an irresistible temptation to its neighbors. The same civil war that tore much of Russia apart quickly enveloped Ukraine. The Poles, Czechs, and Romanians joined in the fray, hoping to take a chunk of rich Ukraine for themselves. For four years, Ukraine saw little but devastation. The elected government finally fled into exile and a Communist government, backed by the Red Army, was installed in Kyiv. Western Ukraine, supported by the Poles and Austrians, held out for a time but finally fell to the new Soviet state in March 1921.

Poland signed a treaty with the new Communist government and once more Ukraine was carved up among the victors, pieces going to Poland, Romania, and Czechoslovakia, with the lion's share to the newly formed Union of Soviet Socialist Republics (USSR). In 1922, Ukraine, along with Belarus, Russia, and Transcaucasia, became one of the first four socialist republics. This federation was controlled by Russia, of course, but the individual republics retained a certain degree of autonomy. In Ukraine, the Ukrainian language could still be spoken and taught in schools, Ukrainian culture was not suppressed, emigrés who had left during the years of civil war were welcomed back, and the Soviet Union's New Economic Policy (NEP) allowed some privately owned businesses to exist.

It looked as though the future of Ukraine might be far better under the Communists than it had been under the czar. But with Lenin's death in 1924, a new leader came to power. He would unleash such terrors on Ukraine that they would make the years under the czars look idyllic. The real nightmare was only beginning.

NOTES

p. 12   "We knew not whether . . ." Robert Wallace, *Rise of Russia* (New York: Time-Life Books, 1967), p. 32.

p. 15   "But my men of Kursk are tried warriors—" Michael Hrushevsky, *A History of Ukraine* (New Haven, Conn.: Yale University Press, 1941), p. 153.

p. 20   "Ukraine is not yet dead . . ." Hodges and Chumak, p. 8.

3

A Soviet Republic

(1924 to 1991)

If Lenin hadn't died of a stroke in 1924, it is entirely possible he would have tightened the reins on Ukraine and the other Soviet republics. But under the dictatorship of Joseph Stalin (1879–1953) such possibilities became certainties.

In 1928, the year he rose to supreme power in the Soviet Union, Stalin abruptly ended the "honeymoon" with Ukraine, his most valued republic after Russia. He reinstated Russian as the official language and banned the use of Ukrainian. He had thousands of artists, writers, and other intellectuals who were opposed to the Soviet government exiled, imprisoned, or executed. Worst of all, in 1929, he set about to collectivize the 25 million peasant farms in the Soviet Union, a large proportion of which were in Ukraine. Once privately run, these farms would now belong to the state, and in many cases the previous owners would become hired laborers on what once was their land.

Stalin, Khrushchev, and the Great Famine

Nowhere was there more resistance to Stalin's collectivization plan than among the stubborn, independent farmers of Ukraine. Most of them refused to send their valuable grain to Russia or give up ownership of their farms. In some cases, farmers put up armed resistance to the Russian soldiers who came to enforce Stalin's will, fighting them with pitchforks and axes. Millions of peasants and their families were forced to emigrate, while others were arrested and executed. Still others were sent to labor camps, which meant lingering deaths. But the worst fate awaited those left behind on the farms.

To punish the Ukrainians for daring to resist him, Stalin requisitioned every ear of grain and even seeds to be exported to Moscow and other cities to feed urban workers. While the workers ate their bread, the peasants of Ukraine went hungry.

The years 1932 and 1933 saw the worst human-caused famine in recorded history. More cruel than nature itself, Stalin caused seven million Ukrainians—men, women, and children—literally to starve to death. This horrendous crime would make Stalin a much hated man in Ukraine and contribute to the defection of tens of thousands of Ukrainians a decade later in World War II.

In 1938, Stalin appointed one of his protégés, Nikita Khrushchev (1894–1971), as first secretary of the Communist Party in Ukraine. Khrushchev was born at *Kalinovka* [Kah-LEE-nov-Kah] on the Ukrainian border, but he knew nothing about agriculture, the lifeblood of Ukraine. He tried to decline the appointment, but Stalin knew Khrushchev's ambition and loyalty made him the right man for the job. Kyiv was a hotbed of nationalism when Khrushchev arrived there, and the working-class leadership was dominated by a liberal intelligentsia.

Khrushchev ruthlessly purged the Communist Party of suspect members. By the summer of 1938, only three of the previous 86 members of the Central

Committee of the Ukrainian Communist Party were still in office. The hunt for "enemies of the state" grew so hysterical that even Khrushchev himself was shocked by the machinery he had put in motion. In his memoirs, he described the accusation of a man named Medved, a respected Ukrainian doctor and deputy chief of the Regional Health Department:

> . . . some woman got up at a Party meeting, pointed her finger at [Medved], and said, "I don't know that man over there but I can tell from the look in his eyes that he's an enemy of the people." Can you imagine?
>
> Fortunately, Medved didn't lose control of himself. He retorted immediately, "I don't know this woman who's just denounced me, but I can tell from the look in her eyes that she's a prostitute"—only he used a more expressive word. Medved's quick comeback probably saved his life. If he'd let himself be put on the defensive and had started protesting that he wasn't an enemy of the people, he would have fallen all the more under suspicion, and the woman who denounced him would have been encouraged to press her charge against him, knowing that she wouldn't have to take any responsibility for what happened.

Interestingly, Medved survived these nightmare years and lived to serve in the Ukrainian delegation that helped found the United Nations in San Francisco in 1945.

The Ravages of War

In 1939, while secretly in league with Nazi Germany, the Soviet Union invaded Poland and carved the country in half. France and Great Britain were aghast and immediately declared war on Germany. World War II had begun. The Soviet Union remained neutral until Germany broke their treaty and attacked Ukraine and other Russian territory in June 1941. Many Ukrainians, suffering under Stalin's harsh rule, welcomed the Germans with open arms. German troops marching into Ukrainian villages were showered with flowers and serenaded by peasants dressed in native folk costumes and playing musical instruments.

Banners hung across arches and read: "The Ukrainian people thank their liberator, the brave German Army. Heil Adolf Hitler!" Some Ukrainians even joined the German cause. Even a patriot such as *Stepan Bandera* [Stch-PAHN Ben-DEH-rah], a leading Ukrainian nationalist, collaborated with the Nazis.

But the Ukrainians had misplaced their hopes. German dictator Adolf Hitler (1889–1945) viewed all Slavs, groups of people with a common heritage, living mostly in Eastern Europe, as *Untermenschen,* meaning "subhumans" in German. Hitler felt they were meant to serve as slaves for his German Reich, their natural resources were to be plundered, and their land was to become homes for German immigrants. The invading Germans treated the Ukrainians with as much contempt as Stalin had.

"There is no Ukraine," boasted Nazi leader Erich Koch, who administered the country with utter cruelty. When a nationalist damaged a

Ukraine was on the front line during the German invasion of the Soviet Union in World War II. By the spring of 1942, the German advance had slowed down to a crawl through a sea of mud from spring rains, as seen here. The Germans were eventually driven out of Ukraine, but by then most of the country's cities and towns were in ruins. (Archive Photos)

German transmitter in Kyiv, Koch ordered 400 men, chosen at random, to be shot. He also had 38,000 citizens of Kyiv deported to Germany in cattle cars to make room for German settlers.

Realizing their mistake, many Ukrainians turned their allegiance back to the Soviet Union. Others, like Bandera, fought both Germans and Russians in an underground nationalist army.

Ukraine became one of the major battlegrounds on the Eastern front, and it was passed back and forth between Germany and Russia, like a football in a hard-fought game. By the war's end in 1945, 6 million Ukrainians were dead; many died in the fighting and others were worked to death in German labor and concentration camps. Ukrainian cities, including Kyiv, lay in ruins, and 18,000 villages were completely destroyed.

Germany's defeat ended the Nazi terror, but the old terror of Stalinism returned as the Soviet Union regained control of Ukraine. Ukrainians returning from German prisons and camps where they had been held prisoner were seen by the paranoiac Stalin as traitors or spies. They were sent to Soviet labor camps or shot. Execution was a certain fate for many collaborators, including thousands of Kozaks.

Ukrainian nationalists continued to fight the Soviets with guerilla tactics. They were led by Bandera, who was now called "Taras Bulba," after the Kozak hero of a story by Ukrainian-born Russian writer Nikolai Gogol (1809–1852). They were crushed only several years later when the Soviets expended all their efforts against them.

A Second Famine

But even those loyal Ukrainians who did nothing to incur Stalin's wrath were not out of harm's way. A second great famine swept the country in 1946. This time nature was the villain. The driest summer on record led to a disastrous harvest, with few farmers left to reap what little grain there was.

Khrushchev, now prime minister of the Ukrainian Soviet Republic, received disturbing reports about death from starvation and even worse. "I read a report that a human head and the sole of feet had been found

The people of Kyiv, many of them in traditional folk costumes, celebrate the 300th anniversary of the reunion of Ukraine with Russia in June 1954. If the smiles on some of the faces seem strained, it may reflect the repression the Ukrainians suffered under Russian and Soviet rule. (UPI/Corbis-Bettmann)

under a little bridge near *Vasilkovo* [Vah-SIL-Koh-voh], a town outside of Kyiv," Khrushchev wrote in his autobiography. "Apparently the corpse had been eaten."

Despite the high death toll, the Ukrainian famine was kept a secret by the Soviets, and even today little is known about it in the West.

Weak and broken though they may have been, Ukrainians clung stubbornly to an ideal of national unity in the postwar years. The Soviet Union seized western Ukraine from Poland and Czechoslovakia. For the first time in centuries, Ukraine was whole, though enslaved.

Following Stalin's death in 1953, there was a scramble for power in the Soviet Union. Nikita Khrushchev emerged the victor by 1956. Khrushchev denounced Stalin for his crimes against the Soviet people, while conveniently overlooking his own participation in those crimes. Ukraine, which Khrushchev knew well from his years as a party leader there, played a central role in his efforts to renew the economy and bring industrial growth. Khrushchev may have been more tolerant than Stalin of Ukrainian culture, but he did not approve of Ukrainian nationalism at Soviet expense and the Russianization of Ukraine continued. It met strong resistance from a small but resilient dissident movement.

The Rise of Brezhnev

Ukraine's importance to the Soviet Union was not just economic, but it was political as well. It produced the next major figure in Soviet politics. Leonid Brezhnev (see boxed biography) hailed from *Dneprodzerzhinsk* [Dneep-ROH-dzer-ZHINSK] (then called *Kamenske* [KAH-mens-Keh]) and worked his way up the Communist Party ladder in Ukraine, becoming a major general on the Ukrainian front during World War II.

Brezhnev was one of Khrushchev's protégés, and the Soviet leader helped him advance through the ranks. Shortly before Stalin's death, Brezhnev was appointed to the party's Central Committee in Moscow. In October 1964, Khrushchev fell from power, mainly because Kremlin leaders disapproved of his economic policies and his antagonistic stand toward Communist China. Brezhnev helped engineer his mentor's fall and within a short time replaced him as Soviet leader.

Although Brezhnev made Ukraine almost a "junior partner" with Russia in the governing of the Soviet Union, his influence was not all to the good. He had little tolerance for any dissent in either the Eastern Europe satellites of the Communist Bloc or within the Soviet Union itself. In 1968, he made the decision to invade Czechoslovakia when its government became too liberal. According to what was called "Brezhnev's doctrine," the Soviet Union had the right, even the duty, to intervene domestically in any Communist-Bloc nation that veered from the strict party line.

As he grew older, Brezhnev relied more and more on his political cronies, many of them from Ukraine, to run the country. Corruption, bribery, and kickbacks became business as usual in the Soviet Union in the 1970s and early 1980s. Government mismanagement wreaked havoc

Leonid Brezhnev (1906–1982)

He called himself a "fifth generation steelman," and he could be as resilient as steel when representing the interests of the Soviet Union. But Leonid Brezhnev could also bend to accommodate the world when it suited his purpose.

Brezhnev was born in a working-class neighborhood of Kamenske, a typical industrial Ukrainian town. His father worked in a steel plant, and he himself worked as a stoker, oiler, and fitter while studying at a local metallurgical institute. Brezhnev became a member of the Communist Party in 1931 and steadily worked his way up the political ladder, achieving the rank of major general in the Red Army during World War II.

After the war, he began working closely with Nikita Khrushchev in Ukraine, becoming his protégé. At the 19th Party Congress in 1952, Brezhnev became a full member of the powerful Central Committee. The death of Stalin, another "man of steel," the following year set back Brezhnev's career temporarily, but as Khrushchev rose to power, he brought Brezhnev along with him. He administered Khrushchev's program of cultivating "virgin lands" in Central Asia and Siberia to improve agricultural productivity.

In 1964, Brezhnev joined other Kremlin leaders in forcing Khrushchev into retirement. Although it was partly Khrushchev's "cult of personality" that led to his removal, Brezhnev later seized power for himself at the expense of his political partner, Alexei Kosygin.

The leader of the Soviet Union for 18 years, Brezhnev was alternatively a stern and indulgent father to Ukraine and the other Soviet republics. He pursued and achieved détente, a relaxing of tensions, with the United States in the early 1970s, but at the same time kept a firm grip on Eastern Europe, invading Czechoslovakia in 1968. He signed numerous nuclear nonproliferation treaties with the United States, but encouraged and supported revolutionary movements in developing nations. In December 1979, he sent Soviet troops into Afghanistan to aid the Communist government, which was there fighting anti-Communist rebels. Afghanistan became the Soviet Union's Vietnam, a disastrous war that dragged on for years after Brezhnev's death.

An adept politician and a skilled negotiator, Brezhnev brought order and security to his country, but he did little to improve the lives of its people. The massive and corrupt bureaucracy he helped perpetuate eventually brought down the Soviet Union and everything he stood for.

Soviet leader Leonid Brezhnev, shown here in a 1977 photo, was Ukrainian by birth and made his homeland a "junior partner" of Russia within the hierarchy of the Soviet Union. The corruption of his last years of power was unfortunately a model for many Ukrainian politicians today.
(UPI/Corbis-Bettmann)

with the once-sturdy Ukrainian economy. This legacy of political corruption would continue to plague the republic of Ukraine even after the collapse of communism.

In November 1982, the 76-year-old Brezhnev died at home of a heart attack. He was replaced in succession by two more Old Guard Communists—Yuri Andropov and Konstantin Chernenko—both of whom were in poor health and died shortly after taking office. In 1985, the Politburo, the governing body of the Soviet Union, chose a younger man as their next leader, one who had new ideas of how to run the Soviet Union.

Mikhail Gorbachev (1931–) promised his people "a thorough renewal of every aspect of Soviet life—economic, social, political and moral." To bring about this renewal he instituted a policy of *perestroika,* the Russian word for "restructuring," that would change and renew old institutions. He also announced a policy of *glasnost,* a "loosening of censorship and government restrictions" in social and cultural life.

Gorbachev's liberal policies gave new hope to the Ukrainian nationalists who had been opposed to Soviet domination for decades. But amid hope, a fresh disaster struck Ukraine.

Chornobyl

On April 26, 1986, an explosion ripped off the top of a nuclear power plant at *Chornobyl* [Chor-NOH-bil], Ukraine, 80 miles north of Kyiv (see boxed feature, chapter 11). The resulting fires took 31 lives. Another 100,000 people were exposed to the high levels of radiation from 11 tons of radioactive particles shot into the air.

In a fatal blunder, the Soviet government waited almost two full days before informing the public of the explosion, the worst civilian nuclear disaster to date. Gorbachev, seeking to distance himself from the tragedy, stayed out of the public eye for almost three weeks. The government dismissed nuclear power officials for negligence and published a detailed report on the disaster and its causes. It also passed strict laws to improve safety in nuclear plants. But the damage had been done.

In the months and years since the accident, thousands of people, many of them children, were struck with cancer, blood diseases, and a host of other illnesses as a direct result of radiation exposure. A radioactive cloud stretched out from the Soviet Union to Sweden, Poland, Finland, and West Germany, poisoning the environment.

The Ukrainians, who suffered most directly from the accident, rose up in anger to protest nuclear power plants in their republic. The protest was so vigorous that it pushed the government to action. Several Soviet reactors, recently completed, were never opened, while others, still being planned, were abandoned.

The Birth of Rukh

Just as Communist governments in Eastern Europe were being besieged by reformers calling for change, people within the Soviet republics were crying for independence, too. Nowhere was the cry for reform louder than in Ukraine. In September 1989, a popular new movement was born. It called itself *Rukh* [ROOKH], meaning "movement" in Ukrainian, and it quickly became the voice of perestroika in the republic. Rukh not only spoke up for political change within Ukraine, but sought a full accounting of the dark past and Stalin's crimes against the Ukrainian people, especially the great famine of 1932–33. In November 1989, Ukrainian Communist Party head Vladymyr *Shcherbitsky* [Shcher-BITS-Kiy] was replaced with the more moderate Vladymyr *Ivashko* [Ee-VAHSH-Koh]. The following March, open elections took place in Ukraine for the first time in nearly 70 years. Members of Rukh and other anti-Communist candidates competed with Communists. The alliance of anti-Communist groups won a fourth of the seats in the parliament, a significant victory.

To dramatize their cause and commemorate the unification of Ukraine in 1919, Rukh organized half a million Ukrainian men, women, and children into a human chain along the highway linking Kyiv and *Lviv* [LVEEV].

Realizing his reforms were threatening to tear apart his nation, Gorbachev proposed a treaty to Ukraine and to the other republics. The treaty would give them some autonomy while reserving other powers for the central government. Ukraine was seriously considering signing this historic union treaty in the summer of 1991, when startling events took place that shook the foundations of the Communist system and made a final break with the Soviet Union inevitable.

NOTES

p. 25   "some woman got up . . ." Nikita Khrushchev, *Khrushchev Remembers* (Boston: Little, Brown, 1970), pp. 114–115.

p. 26   "The Ukrainian people thank their liberator . . ." Nicholas Bethell, *Russia Besieged* (Alexandria, Va.: Time-Life Books, 1977), p. 78.

p. 26   "There is no Ukraine." Bethell, p. 83.

p. 27–28   "I read a report . . ." Khrushchev, p. 234.

4

The Price of Freedom

(1991 to the present)

On Monday, August 19, 1991, the Soviet news media made a stunning announcement: "for health reasons," Mikhail Gorbachev was stepping down from power and passing the reins of government to an eight-man state committee.

In truth, Gorbachev was under house arrest with his family at his Black Sea vacation home. Among the eight conspirators in this coup were antireformers within Gorbachev's very government: his vice president, prime minister, defense minister, and interior minister. They were bent on ending all reforms and returning the Soviet Union to hard-line communism.

Those who opposed the coup, including newly elected President Boris Yeltsin (1931–), gathered at the parliament building in central Moscow. From atop a tank, Yeltsin delivered a defiant speech to a gathered crowd and called for a general strike. Yeltsin supporters took to the streets. The resulting demonstrations frightened the coup leaders into using military force, but it was a halfhearted effort. Two people died in street clashes. Within three days the coup fell apart. One of the conspirators committed suicide, and the others were arrested. Gorbachev was released and returned to Moscow.

The failed coup had a galvanizing effect on the impatient republics within the Soviet Union, nowhere more so than in Ukraine. Not only were the hard-liners shown to be incompetent fools, but so was Gorbachev himself. It was he, after all, who had put the very men who tried to overthrow him in high positions of trust. Here was undeniable proof that communism was dead.

Independence Day

On August 24, days after the coup ended, the Ukrainian parliament, called the Supreme Council, proclaimed its independence from the Soviet Union. The only authority it would hitherto be accountable to was its own

This mass meeting, held in March 1991 in Kyiv, included supporters both for union with the Soviets and Ukrainian independence. Five months later the Supreme Council of Ukraine proclaimed independence from the Soviet Union.
(UPI/Corbis-Bettmann)

constitution and the laws of the land. The day was declared a national holiday, Ukraine's own independence day. The neighboring republics of Belarus and Moldova, along with Uzbekistan and Kyrgyzstan, were quick to declare their own independence. The Soviet Union, after 70 years of existence, was crumbling.

President Yeltsin, acclaimed by the public for his heroic stand during the coup, was at the height of his popularity and took the bold step of outlawing the Communist Party. The Ukrainian leaders knew they could take their cause of freedom to the people with no fear of reprisals from Moscow.

In a national referendum held on December 1, 90 percent of the Ukrainian electorate voted in favor of independence. They simultaneously elected former Communist leader *Leonid Kravchuk* [Leho-NEED Krahv-CHOOK] as their first president. A week later, Ukraine signed the Minsk Agreement with Russia and Belarus. This agreement had a two-fold purpose. It effectively dissolved the Soviet Union as a political entity and joined the three republics in a loose federation they called the Commonwealth of Independent States (CIS). In time, eight other former republics would join this group, roughly the equivalent of the British Commonwealth. The major holdout among the republics was Georgia. Ukraine, a leader in the independence movement, saw the CIS as only an intermediate step on the way to complete independence from Russia and its neighbors.

A Trust Betrayed

But freedom from communism did not mean freedom from other problems. For one thing, Kravchuk, and those who supported him, did not see a break with Russia as an end to privilege for former Communists. Nor did his government believe an independent Ukraine had to follow a strict road to democracy as it was practiced in the West. While the Kravchuk government agreed to work with the reformers of the Rukh national party, they held the upper hand of power and kept real reform at a minimum. Subsidies to state-owned businesses continued and private enterprise was not encouraged.

There was one member of Kravchuk's government, however, who believed reform was inevitable and necessary—Prime Minister Leonid

Leonid Kravchuk was elected the first president of an independent Ukraine in December 1991. His presidency was marred by widespread corruption and foot-dragging on reforms. He was defeated in the June 1994 election by his former prime minister, Leonid Kuchma. (Ellen Shub/Impact Visuals)

Kuchma [KOOCH-mah] (see boxed biography). Kuchma, who was appointed in 1992, backed economic reform and tried to move forward the process of privatization of state companies and industry. One writer called him the "blunt-spoken new prime minister who told white-elephant industries the free ride was over."

It was a message that made him many enemies among the conservative majority in the Supreme Council, the body he oversaw as prime minister. Council members did everything they could to block his reform bills. Frustrated and disenchanted, Kuchma resigned from office in September 1993, leaving Kravchuk to assume many of the powers of the prime minister.

The Ukrainian people, however, were incensed by Kuchma's resignation and blamed it on the government. A general strike was called. The economy, never very healthy since the fall of communism, was plunged into chaos. Under pressure from the public, President Kravchuk was forced to move parliamentary elections up to March 1994 from early 1995.

The Election of 1994

The process of new democratic elections in Ukraine was one of the longest and most torturous in post-Communist Eastern Europe. The new republic had produced a series of complicated election laws that, among other things, required half the electorate to participate and demanded that a candidate had to receive more than half the vote to win. It took nearly five months of runoffs and vote counting to elect 393 of the 450 representatives to the Supreme Council.

The final outcome was surprising. The Communists kept their lead in the parliament with 91 seats, Rukh took 30 seats, and 20 were divided among the remaining political parties. But the largest group of elected representatives—219—were aligned with no political party.

Because the parliamentary elections took so long, Kravchuk postponed the presidential election to June 26. His chief rival was Leonid Kuchma. In two rounds of voting, Kravchuk was defeated by his former prime minister, who got 52 percent of the vote compared to Kravchuk's 45 percent.

President Kuchma set out in the fall of 1994 to achieve several daunting goals: move economic reform forward, end corruption in the government, and make Ukraine new friends abroad. He gave a speech outlining a new economic program in which he vowed to freeze prices, hasten privatization of land and property, and institute a new stable currency, the *hryvnya* [GHRIV-nia]. He also found time to visit Canada and the United States that fall.

The visits abroad were meant to strengthen ties with the West and, more important, get much needed aid and expertise. Following Kuchma's visit, the United States pledged $900 million for the privatization process,

Leonid Kuchma (1938–)

Most Ukrainian politicians spend their lives working their way up the party ladder to achieve power. Leonid Kuchma took a very different road to the top, which he achieved with breathtaking swiftness.

He was born in a small village in Ukraine's *Chernigiv* [CHIRNYE-gif] region. His parents were peasants; his father died during World War II. In 1960, Kuchma graduated from Dnepropetrovsk State University with a degree in mechanical engineering. He soon got a job at *Yuzhavid* [U-ZHOH-veed], the largest missile factory in Ukraine and throughout the world. He would remain there for the next three decades, eventually becoming the company's director in 1986. The company had its own Communist Party Committee, and Kuchma served as its secretary from 1975 to 1982. His political career, however, didn't begin in earnest until 1990, when he was elected to the Ukrainian parliament as a representative from Dnepropetrovsk. He was such an outstanding supporter of economic reform in the newly independent republic that two years later he was appointed prime minister by Ukrainian president Leonid Kravchuk.

The previous prime minister was fired because he failed to initiate economic reform. Kuchma grew increasingly unpopular with conservative parliament members for aggressively pursuing reform. His program to restructure the economy and throw out corrupt officials quickly earned him the title the "iron minister."

But Kuchma could not bend the equally iron will of the legislature. In September 1993, he resigned in frustration. "I am convinced," he said, "Ukraine needs urgent political reforms, without which no economic reforms can occur, and we could well lose our independence."

making Ukraine the third largest recipient of U.S. foreign aid. Canada gave the new nation more than $17 million in technical expertise. The International Monetary Fund said it would give Ukraine $2 billion in loans over a three-year period, but only if it made a sincere and concerted effort toward market reform.

Corruption Widens

Although he had defeated Kravchuk, Kuchma was saddled with the previous president's cabinet ministers and other government workers. Not until March 1995 was he able to overcome resistance in the Supreme Council and appoint his own advisers.

It was the first notice of a new political campaign, this time for president, which he won handily a year later. Kuchma's program for economic recovery included privatizing three-fourths of all state-owned property by 1997, cutting fat subsidies to state-owned businesses, and lifting of price controls.

A strong leader who is not afraid to take a stand and stick with it, Leonid Kuchma may be just the leader Ukraine needs in a time of national crisis.

President Leonid Kuchma spent most of his career as an executive with a missile factory, a career that may have prepared him far better for the presidency than if he had been a career bureaucrat under the Soviet system.
(SHIA photo/Impact Visuals)

Although Kuchma himself was personally untainted by corruption, his election drew many corrupt politicians to his administration. Former acting prime minister *Yuhkim Zvyakilsky* (U-HIM ZVIA-Kil-Skiy] was arrested on charges of embezzlement, and his successor *Yevgeny Marchuk* [Yev-GEN Mar-CHOOK] was later fired for self-promotion. In May 1996, Kuchma appointed *Pavlo Lazarenko* [Pahv-LOH Lah-zah-REN-Koh] as the fifth prime minister since independence.

Lazarenko has proven to be little better than his predecessors. He soon began appointing officials from his home region of *Dnepropetrovsk* [Dneep-ROH-Pet-ROHVSK], where Brezhnev promoted many of his political cronies back in the 1970s. When questioned about this blatant favoritism, Lazarenko replied, "I need my own people."

Even more discouraging, the prime minister helped United Energy Systems, a utility company that he had close ties to, gain a gas distribution monopoly in the region. A controversial figure, Lazarenko was the target of an assassination attempt in July 1996, when a bomb nearly blew up his car as he was riding to the airport.

Lazarenko's abuse of power is only the most visible political corruption. "People are being hired for their loyalty to political factions rather than their commitment to the reform process," said *Slavko Pikhovshesk* [Slahv-KOH Pih-HOV-Shesk], director of the Ukrainian Center for Independent Political Research in Kyiv.

While Kuchma appears to be working for the common good, too many of Ukraine's other leading politicians are looking to get what they can for themselves and for their friends in the rapid changeover to a market economy. The president must do his best to sweep his house clean of this corruption, difficult though it might be.

Trouble in Crimea

Another domestic problem for the Ukrainian president lies to the south. The Crimea, a peninsula of land jutting into the Black Sea, had been given to Ukraine back in 1954 as a goodwill gesture by Nikita Khrushchev. Never in his wildest dreams did Khrushchev think that Ukraine would ever cease to be a part of the Soviet Union and possess the Crimea for itself. This might be said as well for many people living in Crimea, who continue to see themselves as Russians, which many of them are by birth.

When Ukraine became independent in 1991, Crimea's parliament voted to make it an autonomous republic. The Ukrainian republic accepted this, but did not accept a vote for independence from Ukraine in May 1992. The Crimeans persisted. In a runoff presidential election in January 1994, *Yuri Meshkov* [U-riy Mesh-KOHV], a Russian nationalist in favor of separatism, was elected. To further weaken its ties with Ukraine, the Crimean parliament voted to restore the suspended constitution of 1992, which authorized Crimea's sovereignty as an independent power.

In August 1994, the Crimean city of *Sevastopol* [Seh-vahs-TOH-pohl] declared itself a Russian city. Ukraine intervened in March 1995, and a potential rebellion was averted. Over the next two months, Kuchma and the Ukrainian parliament worked tirelessly to bring Crimea back into Ukraine's sphere of influence. They voted to reduce President Meshkov's powers and appointed *Anatoley Franchuk* [Ah-nah-TOH-liy Frahn-CHOOK], Kyiv's man, as the new prime minister. Crimea was calm—for the moment.

A New Day?

For all the troubles facing his country, Kuchma made significant improvements in his first three years as president. By late 1996, most of the economy had been privatized, compared with only five percent when Kravchuk left office in 1994. The average monthly wage had risen in that time from $11 to $80. New treaties with Russia seem to have softened the tension between the two countries.

In May 1997, Russian president Boris Yeltsin made his first trip to Ukraine. Meeting with Kuchma, Yeltsin signed a friendship treaty with Ukraine. Standing at the Tomb of the Unknown Soldier, Yeltsin claimed that Russia's relationship with Ukraine "is a priority of priorities for us. We respect and honor the territorial integrity of Ukraine."

But if tensions with Russia have relaxed, they have not disappeared. Ukraine is still bent on going its own, independent way.

On August 25, 1997, Ukraine celebrated with military exercises the sixth anniversary of its independence from Moscow. Top naval officer Rear Admiral *Mikhaylo Yezhel* [Mih-HI-loh YE-zhel] boldly announced that among the several countries participating in peacekeeping exercises at Donuzlav, the Crimean naval base, would be the United States, bringing two ships with more than one hundred American sailors and marines. Never before had such a U.S. military presence been allowed at the base. It was all part of the North Atlantic Treaty Organization's (NATO) partnership for peace, which Ukraine joined in 1994.

Ukraine's commitment to the West will no doubt cause more problems with Russia, which is still finding it difficult to accept that this former republic, once so important to Russia's welfare, is going its own way. The future may hold problems, but Ukraine, it appears, isn't looking back.

NOTES

p. 38   "blunt-spoken new prime minister . . ." Edwards, "Ukraine: Running on Empty," p. 42.

p. 40   "I am convinced Ukraine needs urgent political reforms . . ." *1997 Current Biography Yearbook* (New York: H. W. Wilson Co., 1997), p. 283.

p. 41   "I need my own people." *Washington Post,* October 27, 1996, CD NewsBank.

p. 42   "People are being hired for their loyalty . . ." *Washington Post,* October 27, 1996, CD NewsBank.

p. 43   "is a priority of priorities . . ." *New York Times,* June 1, 1997, p. 13.

5

Government

Since its independence in 1991, Ukraine has been a nation politically at odds with itself. While it has had its differences with Russia, its internal conflicts have been perhaps even more damaging to its future. Similar to other new nations in Eastern Europe, Ukraine has had to face the double challenge of creating a new market economy while at the same time forging a democratic government that is responsive to the needs of its people.

A Powerful President

Despite its similarities to other Eastern European countries, the government of post-Communist Ukraine is unique in some important ways. Most of its neighbors have followed the English model of a parliamentary system in which the prime minister is the chief executive. In Ukraine, as

Ukraine

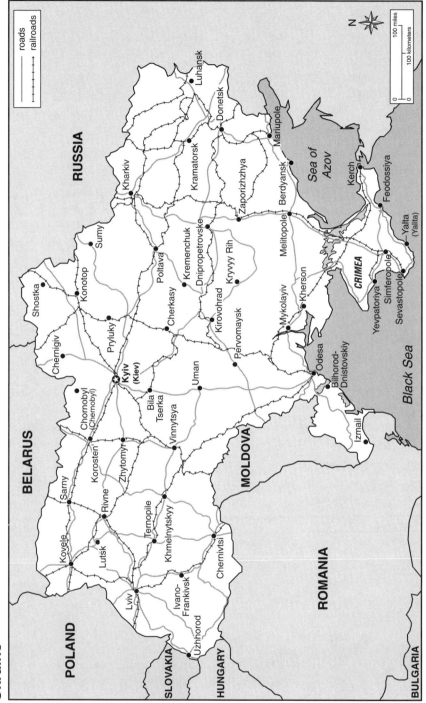

*Russian president Boris Yeltsin (left) welcomes Ukrainian president Kuchma
(right) to Russia. Both men are strong, single-minded leaders who together
have managed to defuse some of the tension between their two countries.*
(Corbis-Bettmann)

in the United States, the president is the chief executive. The Ukrainian
president is the person who signs legislation into law. He is also the
commander in chief of the armed forces.

The prime minister is head of the president's Council of Ministers, which
aids and oversees the president's duties. Members of the council are
nominated by the president and are confirmed by the Ukrainian parliament, *Verkhovna Rada* [Ver-HOV-nah RAH-dah], or Supreme Council.

President Kuchma, who has been in office since June 1994, increased
the presidential powers dramatically a year later by pushing a "constitutional treaty" through the Supreme Council. It gave the president powers
to appoint and dismiss without parliament's approval and gave him the
right to rule by decree when he felt necessary, such as in a national
emergency. A year later, these measures were incorporated in a new
national constitution, which many people felt was long overdue.

Ukraine is one of the few former Soviet republics that did not draft a
new constitution after gaining independence. However, changes were
brought about by Kuchma's new constitution, which also allowed

Ukrainians to own private property, abolished local councils that were against reform, and made Ukrainian the country's official language. The Supreme Council approved the document after an exhaustive 23-hour session on June 28, 1996.

The constitutional changes were not simply the work of a power-mad leader. When he came into office, the Supreme Council blocked Kuchma's every effort to reform the economy and liberalize the government. He was not even able to appoint his own people in government for the first six months in office, but had to contend with those appointments made by his predecessor, Leonid Kravchuk.

If Kuchma can use his new extensive powers wisely to push through his programs without losing the support of the people, he may be in a good position to win reelection in October 1999.

The Supreme Council and the Supreme Court

The power of the Ukrainian legislature has been nearly equal to that of the president. Unlike a number of other Eastern European countries, the parliament here consists of one, not two, houses. The 450 deputies of the Supreme Council serve five-year terms. The current council is dominated by Communists, their allies, and a number of "independents," whose connections to industry and agriculture make them conservative in their outlook. The nationalists and reformers, mainly from western Ukraine, are a vocal minority. In national elections held in March 1998, the Communists won about one-fourth of the vote. Two European monitoring groups criticized the election campaign, claiming it "was marred by incidents of violence, arrests and actions against candidates and abuse of public office."

In a clever move, Kuchma has proposed renaming the Supreme Council the People's Council (*Narodna Rada* [Nah-ROD-nah RAH-dah]), perhaps to make that body more accountable to the people who elected them and not the special interest groups who have made some of them rich. There is also talk of forming a bicameral parliament with two houses that would take away some of the influence of the Supreme Council.

The judicial branch of government is headed by the Supreme Court, which consists of five judges who are elected by the Supreme Council to terms of five years. Again, this court differs significantly from others in the Western world. Constitutional issues, usually the domain of supreme courts, are handled by the Presidium of the Supreme Council, a smaller group within the Council. The Presidium is made up of 19 members, including a chairperson and two vice presidents.

The Ukrainian Supreme Court deals with criminal and civil cases of national importance. "People's Courts," elected by the voters, hear local judicial cases.

National Security

Ukraine's armed forces consists of less than half a million, which does not include the Black Sea fleet. The big question for Russia and Ukraine's friends in the West has been its nuclear weapons. Ukraine was a Soviet stronghold for nuclear weapons prior to independence. Both Russia and the West were nervous about what an independent Ukraine might do with these weapons.

In December 1991, the nuclear weapons were placed under collective CIS control, but this was abolished in 1993, at which time the Ukrainian government laid claim to all nuclear weapons in its territory.

It wasn't until November 1994 that Ukraine signed the Nuclear Non-Proliferation Treaty, agreeing to transfer all nuclear weapons to Russia to be dismantled over a seven-year period. In return, Russia agreed to cancel much of Ukraine's debt. Both the United States and Russia guaranteed Ukraine's future nuclear security.

On June 1, 1996, at a ceremony in south Ukraine, the last nuclear warheads were transferred to Russia. In a symbolic gesture, three defense ministers from Ukraine, the United States, and Russia, planted sunflowers on the site of a former Soviet missile silo.

It has taken longer to settle the issue of the Black Sea fleet. The Russians felt the fleet was theirs, while Ukraine countered that it was on Ukrainian soil and thereby at least partly its possession. After years of frustrated negotiations, the two nations finally reached an agreement in June 1995: Russia would get 82 percent of the fleet, and Ukraine, 18

Soviet nuclear weapons in the hands of Ukraine has been a major issue for both Russia and the West. In a treaty signed in November 1994, Ukraine agreed to transfer all nuclear weapons to Russia to be dismantled. Here, soldiers are loading nuclear tactical weapons onto carrying platforms to be transported to Russia. (Corbis-Bettmann)

percent. Ukraine also gave Russia control of the fleet base at Sevastopol but would be compensated with Russian energy supplies and a further reduction of its debt.

The major issues on defense have been settled. But Ukraine's position between Russia and the West still makes it feel vulnerable. Its future security may be decided by its efforts to become a member of the North Atlantic Treaty Organization (NATO), joining such countries as Poland,

Ukraine's New Diplomatic Corps

To watch the workings of Ukraine's diplomats in Kyiv, you wouldn't know this country's economy was a shambles. These optimists see only good ahead for their country, in spite of its economic difficulties.

Ukraine is enjoying a new and increased status among the world's nations, much of it due to the efforts of Foreign Minister *Hennadiy Udoverto* [Ghen-NAH-deey Uh-doh-VEHR-toh] and his corps of young diplomats. Most of them are bright, single people in their 20s or early 30s who prefer American Pepsi-Cola to Russian vodka, rock music to classical, and Europe to Asia.

"Ukraine wants to return to Europe after hundreds of years in Eurasian space," says Deputy Foreign Minister *Kostyantin Gryshchenko* [Konstian-TIN GHRIH-shchen-Koh]. "This is important to us."

Their biggest coup so far is the broad charter signed with NATO at the Madrid summit meeting in July 1997.

Ironically, the diplomats hold their policy conferences in Kyiv's former Soviet Communist Party headquarters. "In those days, no one could come here," says one young diplomat. "It was a secret world. They said they served the people, but no one would come. Today we're open. That's the difference."

These bold young people seemed determined to make a difference in their country and to see it take its place among the world's nations.

Hungary, and the Czech Republic, who are currently awaiting full NATO membership.

In February 1997, President Kuchma informed his people that the United States and other NATO members had told him that NATO expansion "would not take place without Ukraine's participation." For now that participation is limited to NATO's Partnership for Peace program, a stepping stone to eventual membership.

Foreign Policy

Ukraine's tentative situation with NATO has made for closer relations with other former Soviet republics, especially Georgia. Georgian president Eduard Shevardnadze has supported a stronger political role for Ukraine in the region. He also shares President Kuchma's concern over border disputes both countries have with Russia.

In May 1997, Kuchma and Polish Prime Minister Alexander Kwasniewski signed a "Declaration of Accord and Unity" to end hostile relations between their two nations that go back to the 17th century. More recent conflicts are also being put aside, such as the killing of 35,000 Poles by Ukrainian national insurgents during World War II and the forced resettlement of 150,000 Ukrainians within Poland shortly after the war. Closer ties with Poland and other Eastern European neighbors will gain Ukraine the kind of international recognition it needs to forward its cause with both Russia and the West.

NOTES

p. 48   "was marred by incidents of violence . . ." *New York Times,* April 1, 1998, p. A9.

p. 51   "Ukraine wants to return . . ." *Washington Times,* July 23, 1997, CD NewsBank.

p. 51   "In those days, no one could come . . ." *Washington Times,* CD NewsBank.

p. 51   "would not take place . . ." *Financial Times,* February 19, 1997, CD NewsBank.

6

Religion

"*O*ur church is a wonder to all surrounding lands, and so that the like cannot be found in all the northern lands, nor in the east nor the west," wrote Hilarian, the metropolitan, or archbishop, of the Orthodox Church in Kyiv nearly a thousand years ago.

This was no idle boast. During the time of Kyivan Rus's power, the Orthodox Church was a force to be reckoned with in nearly every area of life. It built monasteries, schools, and poorhouses. It was at the center of Slavic culture and nationhood.

Today, the Ukrainian Orthodox Church remains the largest religion in Ukraine, with 35 million followers. It is a potent symbol of Ukrainian nationalism, even after 70 years of communism.

Perhaps no people in Eastern Europe, outside of the Poles, remain as devoted to their faith as the Ukrainians. Yet, unlike Poland, Ukraine has for centuries had a deep division in its church, brought about, as so many of its problems have been, by the Poles and Russians.

The relationship between the Ukrainian Orthodox Church and the state is clearly illustrated in this scene as an Orthodox priest blesses Ukrainian soldiers with holy water at a military base near Kyiv. The religious holiday Epiphany happened to fall on the same day as an oath-taking ceremony for the soldiers. (Reuters/Yuri Kozakov/Archive Photos)

A Church Divided

The Ukrainian Orthodox Church's power was broken during the Mongol invasion and the subsequent domination of western Ukraine by the Lithuanians and the Poles. Yet it remained the repository of Ukrainian national feelings when there was no political nation. While the Mongols discouraged Christianity in any form, the Poles, devout Roman Catholics, tried to force their brand of Christianity onto the Orthodox Ukrainians. Some converted to Catholicism, but many more resisted.

Realizing that the western Ukrainians would not abandon their religion, the Poles struck a compromise. According to the Union of Brest in 1596, those Orthodox Ukrainians who wished could retain the rites and beliefs of their faith if they would recognize the Roman pope as their spiritual leader. These Ukrainians—both lay people and religious—became known as Ukrainian, or Greek, Catholics.

When western Ukraine was taken over by the Russians after the partition of Poland in the late 18th century, the Ukrainian Orthodox Church was absorbed into the larger Russian Orthodox Church. While the practices and tenets of these two national churches was nearly identical, the Russians saw the nationalism of the Ukrainian church as a threat to their power.

After the Russian Revolution, the newly independent Ukraine republic revived the Ukrainian Orthodox Church. When the republic came under the authority of the Communists a few years later, so did their church. The Communists, avowed atheists, outlawed the Orthodox faith and drove it underground. The Ukrainian Catholic Church, on the other hand, continued to flourish in western Ukraine, which had been taken back by the newly independent Poland.

Poland fell to the Germans in World War II and was taken over, along with western Ukraine, by the Communists in 1946. Ukrainian Catholic priests were accused by the Communists of collaborating with the Nazis and many priests were imprisoned or executed. The Ukrainian Catholic Church was outlawed and its members forced to join the Ukrainian Orthodox Church, which was given some freedom by the Communists. While they did not approve of any church, the Communists felt it would be easier to control one national church than two.

Ukrainian Catholics who continued to worship in their own church did so at great risk. Even children were discouraged from worshiping. Andrew *Palamar* (Pah-lah-MAHR], a 19-year-old from Lviv who is studying at a Ukrainian Catholic seminary in the United States, recalls having a necklace with a cross pulled off his neck by a physical education instructor at school. The incident only strengthened his faith. "You feel it more," he said. "Someone says to you: 'Don't do this.' It makes you want to do it more."

The Ukrainian Church Today

As the Communist state crumbled in Ukraine at the end of the 1980s, the Ukrainian Catholic Church reemerged from the underground. Many Ukrainians were surprised to learn that there were four to seven million church members. In 1990, both the Ukrainian Orthodox Church and the Ukrainian Catholic Church were officially reinstated.

Ukrainian Catholic churches, such as St. George's Cathedral in Lviv, which had been taken over by the Ukrainian Orthodox Church during the Communist era, were returned to the Catholics.

"Serving here is like being beside a person who has awakened from a nightmarish sleep," said Reverend Kenneth *Nowakowski* [Noh-vah-KOVS-Kee], a Ukrainian-Canadian serving at St. George's. "When I came in 1991, people were lined up outside every day. I thought they wanted me to do something for them, but they only wanted to talk. About how they had suffered—just to be heard for the first time."

In August 1992, the leaders of both Ukrainian churches agreed to sit down in Oxford, England, to discuss their differences. Under the name Kyivan Cell Study Group, bishops, priests, and theologians for both churches met to pursue a path toward eventual union. They sought to do this without cutting their ties to either the Roman pope or his Orthodox counterpart, the patriarch, both of whom blessed their mission. If the "Church of Kyiv" can again unite, after four centuries of division, it will be a major step forward for the struggling Ukrainian nation.

But there are other problems facing the Ukrainian Orthodox Church. In September 1996, Russian president Boris Yeltsin signed a religious law singling out the Russian Orthodox Church for special privileges over all other churches in the republics of the former Soviet Union. Shortly after the law came into effect, property owned by the Ukrainian Orthodox Church outside of Moscow, including a cathedral and seminary, was seized by the Russian church.

Ukrainian Orthodox leaders fear the new legitimized power of the Russian Orthodox Church could lead it to dominate them as it once did in the past.

Ukrainian Jews

The Jewish population of Ukraine was substantial up until World War II when hundreds of thousands of Ukrainian Jews perished in Nazi concentration camps or at deportment centers. The worst killing occurred outside Kyiv at a ravine called *Babi Yar* [BAH-beey YAR]. On September 29, 1941, about 35,000 Ukrainian Jews were marched to the ravine and then machine-gunned down by German Nazis. The killing took two days. It is one of the bloodiest massacres in recorded history, and regrettably, local Ukrainian police assisted the Germans.

Today only about 500,000 Jews, one percent of the population of Ukraine, remain. Those who survived the war moved to Israel and elsewhere starting in the 1970s, when the Soviets first allowed them to emigrate.

While Jewish communities are thriving in some cities and synagogues are being reopened, other communities are dying out. In 1989, Rabbi *Moisle-Liev Kolesnik* [Mois-leh-LEE-yev Koh-LES-nik] reopened a synagogue in the border town of *Ivano-Frankivsk* [Ee-VAH-noh-Frahn-KEEVSK], a deportment center for Jews during World War II.

"Every year, two, three or even more families leave, admitted Rabbi Kolesnik. "Most go to Israel, some to the United States or Germany. . . . Most families are mixed. People have lost their traditions. I'm only here because there are still people I can help. Maybe in two years, maybe five, I will have gone, too."

Jewish boys play the American board game of Monopoly during a break at their yeshiva, a Jewish school for higher studies, in Kyiv. There are only about 500,000 Jews in Ukraine today, about 1 percent of the population.
(Sasha Bezzubov/Impact Visuals)

Ukraine's Jewish Mystic

Although he died more than 180 years ago, Rabbi Nachman of Bratslav (1772–1810) continues to exert a powerful influence in his adopted country.

A Jewish mystic who lived and died in the city of *Uman* [UH-mahn], Nachman urged his followers to commune with nature in solitude, a message not unlike that of the Christian Saint Francis.

For a century after his death, Uman was a place of pilgrimage for Nachman's ultra-Orthodox followers, the Bratslav Hasidim. The pilgrimages to his grave site in a Jewish cemetery were stopped when the Communists took over. In 1937, they converted the Uman synagogue into a factory.

In 1988, 250 pilgrims were allowed to visit the rabbi's grave site for the first time in more than 70 years. Since then, the number of pilgrims has swelled, peaking at 7,000 in 1996. The goodwill gesture of the Ukrainian government was partly political. The nation saw it as an opportunity to improve its relations with Israel and bring much-needed revenue to Ukraine. However, a recent incident may cause them to rethink this policy.

In November 1996, two young fanatical followers of Rabbi Nachman attempted to dig a tunnel under the graveyard, steal his corpse, and return it to Jerusalem. They were caught and sent back to Israel.

The Ukrainian government does not want to end the pilgrimages to Uman, but it is concerned about security at the old and historic Jewish graveyard where Nachman is buried. This problem is another example of how politics affects religion in this land of many religions.

Other Religious Groups

There are some 200 Roman Catholic parishes in Ukraine, mostly composed of Poles and Hungarians living in western Ukraine. Since communism's fall, several Protestant denominations have made serious inroads in Ukraine. The two biggest are the Ukrainian Baptist Church and the Ukrainian Evangelical Alliance.

The Crimea is home to Ukraine's small Muslim population. This area was part of the Turkish Ottoman Empire from the 1400s to 1783, when it was annexed by the Russians. Despite periods of persecution and indifference, the Muslims of the Crimea have remained devoted to their faith and send their children to Islamic schools.

While the Ukrainian Orthodox Church remains the religion of a majority of Ukrainians, as many as 60 different religions have adherents in Ukraine. Hopefully this tolerance, in conjunction with strong spiritual values, will help Ukrainians find a moral center that was partially eroded during seven decades of Communist rule.

NOTES

p. 53   "Our church is a wonder . . ." Wallace, p. 32.

p. 55   "You feel it more . . ." *Sunday New York Times,* December 1, 1996, Connecticut section, p. 8.

p. 56   "Serving here is like being beside a person who has awakened . . ." Edwards, "Ukraine: Running on Empty," p. 52.

p. 57   "Every year, two, three or even more . . ." *Financial Times,* Scripps Howard News Service, July 29, 1996, CD NewsBank.

7

The Economy

Since earliest times, Ukraine has been blessed with fertile soil, a temperate climate, rich natural resources, and a people for whom technology has always held a strong attraction. Outside of Russia, no republic within the Soviet Union contributed so much to the Soviet economy. Yet in the post-Soviet era, despite all these advantages, Ukraine's economy has stumbled and fallen. This chapter will present the reasons for this failure, while looking at the strengths and weaknesses of the Ukrainian economy, both past and present.

The Soviet Union's Economic Mainstay

It is no exaggeration to say that the Soviet Union could not have survived without the economic wealth of Ukraine. This one republic supplied the Soviets with one-fourth of their industrial product, one-fourth of all their

This marketplace in Kyiv is one of the few places left where city dwellers can find food at reasonable prices. As this woman's expression reveals, the economy is not good for either seller or buyer. (Fabienne Bouville/Impact Visuals)

agricultural produce, one-third of all meat, one-half of all iron ore, and one-third of all steel.

All of this abundance both helped and hurt Ukraine. On one hand, it gave Ukraine special status among the republics, even, at times, special privileges that others did not enjoy. On the other hand, the system of Soviet central management that distributed all goods was costly and wasteful. Much of the riches from factories and farms were funneled elsewhere in the nation and neither fed nor profited Ukrainians. Amid fields of ripe crops, Ukrainian peasants too often went hungry. Those few who did reap riches were the corrupt Communist officials and politicians, the legacy of the Brezhnev era.

When Ukraine broke with the Soviet Union and announced its independence, it was with the hope that it would establish a free open-market economy, independent of the Soviet system. But the subsequent breakup of the Soviet Union hurt Ukraine nearly as much as it did Russia. The two republics depended heavily on one another.

Breadbasket of the Commonwealth

The southern Ukraine is the steppe, a region covered by short grasses that receive only 10 to 20 inches (25 to 50 cm) of rain a year. The steppe has a rich, black soil called chernozem that is perfect for raising crops, especially grains such as wheat, rye, flax, and barley. The grassland is ideal for livestock grazing. Irrigation of the steppes has led to the growth of fruit trees and vegetables such as tomatoes, peppers, and melons.

The grain of the Ukraine has been used to make the bread that fed millions in the Soviet Union. It earned the region the name the Breadbasket of the Soviet Union and more recently, the Breadbasket of the Commonwealth of Independent States.

The northern Ukraine is also important agriculturally. The cooler climate and less fertile soil is excellent for producing potatoes, rye, flax, and sunflowers. The seeds of the sunflowers are eaten by animals and people or crushed for their rich oil. Dairy cattle are raised in the north and beef cattle in the south, where there are more natural pastures for grazing. Other important livestock includes pigs, sheep, goats, and poultry.

The state farms and collective farms of the Soviet era still exist, but they are gradually being phased out. Agricultural production has been contracted out to smaller private farms, mostly family owned. Since the Gorbachev era, the family farmers have been encouraged to expand the operation of gardens, fruit orchards, and livestock. The state farms have administrated the work, but dismantling this elaborate system can only be done at great cost.

Many young people, such as *Ihor Mychajlyshyn* [EE-ghor Mih-hi-LIH-shin], who now lives in Lviv, have left the family farms. "The people who knew how to farm are the old ones," he explained. "People like me might go back, but we don't know how to work the land. Anyway, there's hardly any equipment."

Treasures from the Earth

If the Ukraine soil is rich, what lies under it is just as precious. Few nations in the world have as much mineral wealth. Mining, an industry here for

A Coal Miner's Life

In the rich coal mines of the Donets Basin near Donetsk, coal mining is a way of life with a long and proud tradition. Before independence, the Donets Basin produced one-third of the coal for the Soviet Union.

generations, produces vast amounts of coal, iron ore, and manganese ore used in manufacturing steel and cast iron. Other valuable minerals include aluminum, titanium, graphite, marble, gemstones, and the most precious of metals, gold. Salt deposits are, in some places, more than 600 feet (183 m) thick. It is doubtful Ukraine will ever run out of this useful mineral.

Clay is also mined and used in everything from pottery to soap. One kind of pure white clay, called kaolin, is used in high-grade ceramics, medicines, textiles, and a coating for paper.

Oil is produced in the western foothills of the Carpathian Mountains and refined at Lviv and *Drogabych* [Droh-GHOH-bich]. Natural gas is produced at *Dashera* [DAH-Sheh-rah] and *Shebeliska* [Sheh-beh-

Today, coal miners are among the highest paid workers in Ukraine. "The money isn't the only thing," says miner Viktor *Anatoly* [Ah-nah-TOH-liy]. "My father and grandfather were coal miners. We're a dynasty."

Well paid as they are, these miners earn their money. Each day, they travel down mine shafts often more than 2,000 feet (610 m) deep. Once at the bottom, they may find themselves walking to a coal site scrunched over under a four-foot-high (1.2 m) ceiling, the only light coming from their helmet lamps. The presence of flammable methane gas is a constant threat, and miners never carry anything capable of a making a spark for fear of igniting the air.

Much of the anthracite coal has been removed in these mines, and extracting what's left can be difficult. Miners often use large cutting wheels to slice off the coal, another job hazard. Then there's the occupational diseases, such as bronchitis and black lung, that they can contract.

Despite these drawbacks, the miners of the Donets Basin continue to go about their important work of providing coal and energy for their nation.

Opposite: *Coal miners are among the highest paid workers in Ukraine today. These miners are going down the shaft in an elevator at Butovka-Donastkaya coal mine.* (Reuters/Corbis-Bettmann)

LEEN-Kah]. Both these energy resources are limited. Ukraine has found itself having to import fuel from other countries within the CIS. Uranium deposits have been used to fuel nuclear reactors, but the disaster at Chornobyl has called into question the future of nuclear power as an energy source in the country (see boxed feature in chapter 11).

A Corrupt Regime

After declaring their independence, the Communist leaders of Ukraine, although no longer under orders from Moscow, continued to use their positions of power for private gain. Only now, the pickings under the process of privitization were much more attractive. Officials and politicians in control of most of the businesses could make capitalism work for themselves—and no one else.

Western businesses were interested in gaining a toehold in Ukraine but were quickly disillusioned. Corrupt officials favored Ukrainian businesses over foreign ones and drove out many investors and businesspeople from abroad. Top U.S. companies, such as Motorola, have abandoned plans to open businesses in Ukraine.

"The government is constantly changing the rules of the game," said American businessman Joseph Lemire. "There is no desire by the Ukrainian government to ever have foreign investment."

Those foreign businesses that have tried to stick it out and stand up to the corruption have been threatened with violence, even death. "It's all rooted in one thing," claimed American businessman David Swure, "total, unequivocal corruption."

While the average worker scrapes by on about $30 a month in wages, officials and politicians have sent perhaps $100 billion in profits into foreign bank accounts. President Kuchma, who has condemned the corruption and is not a part of it, has only begun to eradicate it. Even some of his own advisers, it is believed, are "on the take."

The Future

Since coming to power, President Kuchma has accelerated economic reform in every sector of society. He has pushed mass privatization, drastically cut subsidies to industry, lifted price controls and rents, and removed controls on exports and currency. The country is beginning to get its breath back. Inflation is under control, and employment is up. Foreign aid, if not foreign investments, is making a difference. Despite misgivings in some quarters, the United States continues to support Ukraine. But to gain the expertise and business from abroad that it needs to continue to improve the economy, Ukraine must clean up the corruption and create a friendly environment for investors and businesses. It may be many years before the Ukrainian economy is as healthy as those in Western democracies, and even in some Eastern European ones, but the government is finally making a genuine effort. And that bodes well for the future.

NOTES

p. 63   "The people who knew how to farm . . ." Edwards, "Ukraine: Running on Empty," p. 52.

p. 65   "The money isn't the only thing . . ." Edwards, "Ukraine," p. 617.

p. 66   "The government is constantly changing . . ." *New York Times,* April 9, 1997, p. A3.

p. 66   "It's all rooted in one thing . . ." *New York Times,* p. A3.

8

Culture

The 1990s have been an exciting time for Ukrainian culture. After centuries of suppression and neglect under Polish, Russian, and Soviet domination, the rich traditions of Ukrainian culture are being revived everywhere. Ukrainian language classes across the country are filled with eager students. Ukrainian folklore, folk art, and folk music are more popular than ever. National plays and operas are performed frequently. The Ukrainian people are celebrating their heritage as they seek a national identity denied them for much of their history.

However, separating what is Ukrainian from what is Russian in this culture is not always easy. For many years, Ukrainian writers, artists, and composers were identified as Russian, and some are still so today. Yet many of these creative artists remained Ukrainian in their bold styles and unique perspectives. As the Ukrainian cosmonauts have conquered space, these artists have often been pioneers in exploring new styles and ways of expressing themselves.

Language

Ukrainian is one of the Eastern Slavic languages and is, not surprisingly, very similar to Russian. For centuries, Russian was the official language of the country, but the Russians could no more stamp out the Ukrainian language than they could the spirit of the people who continued to speak it. Today, Ukrainian is spoken by 73 percent of the population, while 22 percent speak Russian. Many people speak both languages.

The Ukrainian government has worked tirelessly since independence to promote Ukrainian, providing language classes for those rusty in its use. Many people, including foreigners, have had to get used to seeing for the first time the Ukrainian—and not the familiar Russian—names of places and people. For example, the capital city is no longer the Russian "Kiev" but the Ukrainian "Kyiv."

Literature

Eastern Slavic literature, as with much of Slavic culture, was born in Kyivan Rus. Great works of religion, history, and epic tales make up the bulk of these earliest writings. The oldest literary classic, dating back to the 10th century, is the *Tales of Bygone Years,* the definitive chronicle of early Ukrainian history. There is also Abbot *Danylo's* [Dah-NIH-loh] vivid description of his two-year journey to the Holy Land in 1106 and the epic *Lay of Igor's Campaign,* written about the same time.

The Mongol invasion in the 1200s abruptly ended the flowering of Ukrainian literature for several centuries. The oral tradition, however, persisted where the printed word disappeared. The Kozaks in the 16th century created their own literary tradition with heroic songs of their exploits, called *dumy* [DOO-my]. The same century saw the first printing presses in Ukraine and the first printed books, including the Gospels of the New Testament and a dictionary. While these first books were written in Ukrainian, later works were mostly written in Russian, the language of Ukraine's new masters.

By the 19th century, such great Ukrainian writers as Nikolai Gogol, Anton Chekhov (1860–1904), and Fyodor Dostoevsky (1821–1881), who was half Ukrainian, were identified as Russian writers and still are by most people today.

In at least one work, however, Gogol celebrated his Ukrainian ancestry. His short novel *Taras Bulba* (1835) takes place during the fierce war between Kozaks and Poles in the 17th century. It is the tragic story of the Kozak leader Taras Bulba, who is betrayed by a son who falls in love with a Polish girl. Interestingly, Gogol's own ancestor, Kozak *Ostop Gogol* [OS-TAHP GOH-gol], went over to the Polish side during this same turbulent period. In the novel's climax, Taras faces death bravely at the hands of the Poles as he watches his men escape:

> From his lofty post of observation he could see everything, as in the palm of his hand.
>
> "Take possession, my lads, take possession quickly," he shouted, "of the hillock behind the forest: they can't approach it!" But the wind did not carry his words to them. "They'll perish, perish for nothing!" he said, in despair, and glanced down to where the Dnyeper [Dnipro] gleamed. Joy shone in his eyes. He descried the sterns of four boats peeping out from behind the bushes; and he gathered together all the strength of his voice, and shouted in a ringing tone: "To the shore, to the shore, my lads! descend the path on the left, under the cliff. There are boats on the strand; seize them all, that the foe may not catch you!"
>
> This time the breeze blew from the other quarter, and all his words were audible to the kazaks [Kozaks]. But for this counsel he received a blow on the head with the butt-end of an axe, which made everything dance before his eyes. . . .
>
> When Taras Bulba recovered from the blow, and glanced at the Dnyeper, the kazaks were already in the skiffs, and were rowing away. Bullets showered upon them from above, but did not reach them. And the old Ataman's eyes sparkled with joy.
>
> "Farewell, comrades!" he shouted to them from above; "remember me, and come hither again next spring to make merry!—What if ye have captured me, ye devilish Lyakhs? Think ye that there is anything in the world which the kazak fears?"

The most prominent and influential Ukrainian writer of the 19th century was Taras Shevchenko. Shevchenko was born a serf and, after being orphaned, was brutally abused as a child by a church caretaker who

Lesya Ukrayinka (1871–1913)

The life of this great Ukrainian writer is a study in determination and courage. She was born *Larisa Kvita-Kosach* [Lah-RIH-sah KVEE-tah-KOH-sahch] into a family of intellectuals. Her mother was a well-known writer and her father a prominent patron of the arts. At the age of 10, she was stricken with tuberculosis and spent much of her adult life traveling the globe in search of a cure.

Ukrayinka began writing poetry at the age of nine. Her first volume of poems, *On the Wings of Songs* (1893), was highly praised by critics. By the time her third book of poetry appeared in 1902, she was regarded as the leading Ukrainian poet of her generation.

Despite all her traveling, Ukrayinka never forgot her homeland and even took it as her pseudonym. Her passion for Ukraine did not, however, limit her scope as a writer. She was the first Ukrainian playwright to set her works in other places and times, including the Middle Ages, biblical times, and colonial America. On another level, though, most of her plays dealt with problems and issues facing the men and women of her country. She was also a prolific translator, producing Ukrainian versions of everything from the plays of Shakespeare to Egyptian folk songs.

Ukrayinka died before seeing her land free, yet her writings expressed feelings and emotions that helped fuel the fight for Ukrainian independence.

Lesya Ukrayinka is one of Ukraine's most revered modern writers. This statue of her by Mychajlo Chereshniovsky was erected in Toronto in 1975 by the Ukrainian Canadian Women's Committee.
(The Ukrainian Academy of Arts and Sciences in the U.S.A.)

adopted him. He apprenticed himself to mural painters and exhibited a gift for painting. A group of intellectuals were so impressed with his talent that they paid for his freedom. Later, Shevchenko joined a nationalist organization and begin writing powerful tracts condemning the Russian regime and urging Ukrainian independence. For these works he was exiled to Central Asia for 10 years. Here in lonely isolation, romantic poetry and novels poured out of the writer. Ironically, Shevchenko, the champion of freedom, died a week before the czar emancipated all serfs, but his work continued to influence Ukrainian writers and artists for decades.

Shevchenko's legacy lived on in the works of two writers—*Ivan Franko* [Ee-VAHN Frahn-Koh] (1856–1916) and *Lesya Ukrayinka* [LEH-sia UhK-rah-YIN-Kah] (see boxed biography). Franko was one of Ukraine's most celebrated and prolific writers. His harsh, realistic novels such as *Boa Constrictor* (1878), vividly depicted the plight of Ukrainian workers and peasants under Russian rule. Franko's works number more than 1,000 and include poetry, plays, histories, and criticism.

Ukrayinka, like Shevchenko, spent years in exile, but voluntarily. She lived abroad to recuperate from tuberculosis. Her poems and plays are noted for their sublime lyricism and use of Ukrainian folklore and mythology.

Both these writers died before the Soviet takeover, a fate that destroyed the careers of many writers who followed them. During the brutal Stalin years, many writers were killed, imprisoned, or deported.

Despite the fact that they might never return home, exiled writers clung to their national identity. In the 1950s, emigrés in the United States formed the Ukrainian Writers' Association in Exile, called *Slavo* [SLAH-voh].

Meanwhile, back in Ukraine, many writers secretly shared among each other manuscripts to be read and discussed. Many of these works were later smuggled out of the Soviet Union and published in Western countries.

Since independence, Ukrainian writers are free to express themselves however they choose to. Poetry continues to be one of the most popular literary genres, along with science fiction. Exploring new worlds continues to be a preoccupation among Ukrainian authors.

Music

When most people think of Ukrainian music, they picture a robust male chorus singing folk songs or colorfully dressed folk dancers leaping into the air doing the dance called the *hopak* [Ghoh-PAHK], meaning "grasshopper" in English.

The folk music of Ukraine goes back to Kozak times and earlier. Many songs and ballads are traditionally sung a cappella, without accompaniment. Others are accompanied by the *bandura* [bahn-DOO-rah], a stringed folk instrument that resembles a lute.

There is also a long tradition of classical music in Ukraine. Nationalistic operas, such as *A Kozak Beyond the Danube* (1863) by composer *Semen Hulak-Artemovsky* [Seh-MEN Ghoo-LAHR-Ahr-teh-MOVS-Kiy], continue to be performed today. The Kyiv Chamber Choir, founded in 1990, specializes in both ancient and modern liturgical works. When the 20-voice choir sang at New York's Carnegie Hall in 1997, one reviewer praised their "disciplined, well-blended sound that was appealingly varied in color . . ."

Ukraine has six opera houses, nine symphony orchestras, and seven chamber orchestras. Jazz and rock music are also popular.

Art and Architecture

Ukrainian architecture was the glory of Kyivan Rus in its golden age. Ornate churches made of wood with towering spires, brilliant mosaics, and ornate carvings are today preserved as museums, although some of the finest were torn down by the Soviets in their campaign to quash Ukrainian nationalism. One church, the Cathedral of St. Sophia in Kyiv, was saved from such a fate only by the protest of many nations.

Icon painting was a dominant art form for centuries in Ukraine, and these religious paintings, made with egg tempura on wooden panels, were so beautiful that they were once thought to have miraculous powers.

By the 17th century, the influence of Western Europe led Ukrainian artists to turn to such forms as sculpture and portrait painting. Taras Shevchenko created a school of realism that flourished in the 19th century. The early 20th century saw a number of powerful Expressionistic artists who captured in their art the stark tragedy of their homeland in modern history.

But the most influential and important Ukrainian artist of the 20th century was sculptor *Oleksandr Arkhypenko* [Oh-lek-SAHNDR Ahr-HIH-pen-Koh] (1887–1964), known in Russian as Alexander Archipenko. Arkhypenko was born in Kyiv and moved to Paris as a young man to pursue his art. He took the technique of Cubist painting, which turned everyday objects and people into geometric shapes, and brilliantly adapted it to sculpture. He moved to the United States in 1923 with his wife, at that time speaking only a few words of English.

"America fires my imagination more than any other country," Arkhypenko said soon after his arrival, "and embodies more of that flexibility, that yeastiness, which means life and vitality and movement."

Arkhypenko's sculptures have all three of these qualities and can be seen today in many American museums. He was as great a teacher as he was an artist and founded his own art school as well.

Folk Arts

Folk art holds a special place in Ukrainian culture. Even the most humble wooden dwelling is adorned with elaborate carvings on the doors and windows. In previous decades, every peasant home proudly displayed at least one icon. Elaborate, colorful cross-stitching adorns everything from folk costumes to tablecloths.

Perhaps the most honored folk art is *pysanky* [PIH-sahn-Ki], the art of painting colored Easter eggs by using melted wax and dyes. Images painted on the eggs have symbolic meanings. Trees, for example, represent long life, and birds, fertility. Other images may stand for the creator's life and profession. Some Ukrainian Easter eggs are so exquisitely designed that they are family heirlooms, passed down from generation to generation.

Theater

The theater came rather late to Ukraine, but it quickly became a popular art form. Historical dramas and puppet plays were popular in the 17th and 18th centuries. Actor-playwright *Marko Kropyvorytsky* [MAHR-Koh Kro-piv-NITS-Kiy] (1840–1910) established the first permanent theatrical troupe in the late 1800s. The plays his troupe performed in villages and towns were often historical dramas featuring flawless heroes, beautiful heroines, and snarling villains.

More mature dramas were written in the early 20th century by Ivan Franko, for whom a famous Kyiv theater is named, and Lesya Ukrayinka, who specialized in poetic drama.

The painting of Easter eggs, called pysanky, *is a fine art in Ukraine. This woman has a difficult time choosing an egg to buy from this dazzling display outside St. George's Cathedral in Lviv.* (Reuters/Corbis-Bettmann)

After World War I and independence in 1918, Ukraine experienced a flowering of theater, led by *Les Kurbas* [LES KOOR-bahs] (1887–1942), who founded the *Berezil* [Beh-reh-ZEEL] Theater, and his protégé playwright *Mykola Kulish* [Mih-KOH-lah Koo-LEESH] (1892–1942). Kulish's expressionistic plays were seen as ugly by authorities, and many were banned. Kurbas was killed in a Stalinist purge, and Kulish was arrested and sent into exile. It was the end of meaningful theater for many years.

Nevertheless, some playwrights managed to circumvent the Soviet censors, such as *Oleksandr Levada* [Oh-lek-SAHNDR Leh-VAH-dar] (1909–), whose space-age version of the Faust legend was produced in 1960.

Today the theater is alive and well in post-Communist Ukraine, with 60 professional theaters performing regularly. There are also elaborate puppet theaters in every major city.

Film

If you should go to a movie theater in Ukraine, be forewarned. There is no eating popcorn during the movie and talking is strictly forbidden. Ukrainians love the cinema, but they are terribly serious about movies, and for good reason.

The Soviet cinema was one of the most original in the world in the 1920s, and Kyiv was a center of filmmaking. Ukrainian *Oleksandr Dovzhenko* [DOV-ZHEN-Koh] (see featured biography) was one of the greatest filmmakers of this era. Dovzhenko's early silent films, including *Zvenigora,* [Zveh-NIH-goh-rah] *Arsenal,* and *Earth,* are intensively lyrical and express the director's deep love for his homeland and its peasants.

Dovzhenko's passion for Ukrainian folklore and legend lives on in the work of such filmmakers as *Serky Paradzhon* [Sehr-KIY Pah-rah-DZHAHN], whose *Shadows of Forgotten Ancestors* (1964) was an international success.

A disruptive economy and the loss of the state support enjoyed under the Soviet system has made it difficult for many creative artists in Ukraine to get financial backing for their work. But artists, writers, and composers continue to keep alive a tradition that draws heavily on both a rich folk heritage and the individual spirit of its creators.

Oleksandr Dovzhenko (1894–1956)

Until he was 32, the greatest of Ukrainian filmmakers never set foot in a film studio or, for that matter, never saw more than a few films. "You could say that I stood a naked man on the Black Sea coast," Oleksandr Dovzhenko later wrote about his arrival at the Odesa Film Studio. "In the thirty-third year of my life I had to start learning all over again."

But then Dovzhenko had been facing challenges all his life. He was born in abject poverty in the town of Sosnitsa [SOS-neet-sah], where his father was an illiterate peasant farmer who could barely make a living. Of the family's 14 children, only Dovzhenko and a sister survived to adulthood. She became a doctor, and he, a science teacher at age 19. He soon became involved in politics and worked in foreign embassies for the Soviet government before returning to Kyiv as a cartoonist and book illustrator.

Two years after arriving at the Odesa studio, he directed his first film masterpiece, *Zvenigora* (1928). As with all his great films, it had little plot but incredible atmosphere and feeling derived from the history and folklore of his native Ukraine.

But despite his artistic greatness, Dovzhenko was criticized by Soviet critics for making eccentric and indulgent films. Disillusioned with the impossible working conditions the government imposed on him, he turned increasingly away from films and spent his time writing short stories and novels.

During World War II, Dovzhenko worked as a war correspondent and witnessed the destruction of his beloved Ukraine. He wrote a film scenario, *Ukraine in Flames,* that Stalin disapproved of. The Soviet dictator was furious with Dovzhenko's nationalism and had him fired from the Kyiv Studio.

Disillusioned and bitter, Dovzhenko died at age 62 of a heart attack. He never lived to film his dream project, a movie of Gogol's Kozak novel, *Taras Bulba.*

Opposite: *Oleksandr Dovzhenko came from a peasant family, and the folkways and lyric beauty of the Ukrainian countryside infuse his films, which are among the greatest in early Soviet cinema.* (The Ukrainian Academy of Arts and Sciences in the U.S.A.)

NOTES

p. 71   "From his lofty post of observation . . ." Nikolai Gogol, *Taras Bulba: A Tale of the Cossacks* (New York: Knopf, 1931), pp. 282–284.

p. 74   "disciplined, well-blended sound . . ." *New York Times,* December 23, 1997, p. E5.

p. 75   "America fires my imagination . . ." Donald H. Karshan, editor, *Archipenko: International Visionary* (Washington, D.C.: Smithsonian Institution Press, 1969), p. 103.

p. 78   "You could say that I stood . . ." John Wakeman, editor, *World Film Directors, Vol. 1 (1890–1945)* (New York: H.W. Wilson, 1987), p. 261.

9

Daily Life

---

*F*or all the promise of this potentially wealthy republic, life in Ukraine today is difficult for the vast majority of its citizens. Wages are low (averaging $30 a month), inflation is still high, crime is rampant, and the government is riddled with corruption.

The hope for Ukraine, as with most nations, lies in the next generation that will one day run the country, hopefully better than their elders have. Education is the key for today's youth, and Ukraine's educational system is one of the best in Eastern Europe.

Education

Education has a long and revered history in Ukraine. It was one of the first countries in Europe to educate girls as well as boys, although only the nobility in early times sent its children to school. The Mongols ended national education, while the Poles later replaced Ukrainian schools with Catholic schools run by Jesuits. Metropolitan *Petro Mohyla* [Pet-ROH Moh-GHIH-lah], the great Orthodox religious leader, founded the

Kyiv-Mohyla [KIH-yeevs-Moh-ghih-LAH] Academy in 1633. This innovative institution of higher learning was open to young scholars from all classes, something unheard of in Europe at the time. Mohyla also encouraged young people to study abroad as part of their education, another new concept in learning.

The Russians shut down the Kyiv-Mohyla Academy in 1817, and it became a seminary for Orthodox priests. New universities were thoroughly "Russified," with the Ukrainian language forbidden to be spoken and Ukrainian culture forbidden to be taught.

When the Soviets took over, education became compulsory for all youth. Also, universities and other institutes of higher learning were free to any student who qualified. But what Ukrainians were learning in the classroom was often controlled and twisted. The great Academy of Science of Ukraine, founded in 1918 under the Ukrainian republic, was corrupted by Communist doctrine and became largely a tool of the Soviets. However, important strides were made in certain scientific fields. For example, Ukrainian scientists and cosmonauts were in the forefront of the Soviet space program.

Today Ukraine continues to lead the world in such areas of scientific research and discovery as oceanography. Research ships stationed in Odesa and Sevastopol study marine biology and conduct experiments in the desalinization of seawater.

One positive legacy left by the Soviet era is universal education. Students must attend school for eight years—four years of elementary school and four of secondary school. Upon finishing the eighth grade, they have several choices. They can continue public school for three more years, go to a trade school for two years of job training, or immediately go to work. Those who complete secondary school may apply to one of Ukraine's nine universities; special-interest colleges for careers in agriculture, music, and other fields; or one of the country's many technical colleges.

In 1992, the Kyiv-Mohyla Academy reopened, more than 175 years after the Russians closed its doors. It is the first non-state-run university in Ukraine. And so a great educational tradition continues into the 21st century.

Women's Roles

While many young women can receive a good education in Ukraine, their chances of finding a decent job after graduation are slim. As in Russia and other former Soviet republics, women are often the first to be fired in layoffs and job cutbacks. Two-thirds of all unemployed people in Ukraine are women. Those women who are professionals, such as teachers and doctors, are poorly paid even by Eastern European standards.

Yet at the same time, Ukrainian women, especially in the rural areas, have more freedom to live as they choose than ever before.

"Girls now have few opportunities yet great freedom . . ." said *Olga Shved* [OL-gah SHVED], who runs a center in Kyiv dedicated to combating the illegal trafficking of women in Eastern Europe. "Here the towns are dying. What jobs there are go to men. So they leave."

As many as 400,000 women under 30 have left Ukraine in the past 10 years. Many go to Israel, Turkey, or Germany, lured by advertisements for high-paying jobs. Most of these ads are fronts for the growing international sex trade.

In 1996, Lena, an 18-year-old, high school–educated girl from a Ukrainian village, answered a newspaper ad and applied for a good-paying job as an orange picker in Cyprus. The agency who paid for her airfare, however, sent her to Turkey instead, where she was forced to work as a prostitute in a hotel for nine months before finally managing to escape with the help of the Ukrainian embassy.

Other women seem more resigned to their new lives. Tamara, a 19-year-old Ukrainian, works in a massage parlor in Tel Aviv, Israel. She admits "I'm not sure I would go back now if I could. What would I do there, stand on a bread line or work in a factory for no wages?"

Until economic conditions improve and women can see a future for themselves in Ukraine, they will continue to emigrate, many to be victimized in other countries.

Sports and Recreation

For decades, Ukraine has turned out some of the finest athletes in the world, but few people realized it. In the Olympic Games and other international competitions, Ukrainian athletes competed under the banner of the Soviet Union. Not anymore. Ukraine now takes great national pride in such Olympic gold-medal champions as figure skaters *Viktor Petrenko* [VEEK-tor Pet-REN-Koh] and *Oksana Baiul* [OK-SAH-nah Bi-OOL] (see

Oksana Baiul (1978–   )

In many ways, she is the Cinderella of figure skating, but so far her fairy tale has no happy ending. Oksana Baiul was born in a grim Ukrainian factory town. When she was two, her parents divorced and her father left them. Her mother encouraged her ice skating but died of

cancer when Oksana was 13. The next year, Oksana's skating coach moved to Canada without telling her. Angry and bitter, Oksana threw her skates in the trash and vowed she would never skate again. Fortunately, she didn't keep that promise.

Skating on her own, Oksana met the great Ukrainian skating coach *Galina Zmiuoskaya* [Gah-LIH-nah Zmee-YEV-Skah]. Galina agreed to become her coach and invited the orphan girl to move into her home. Here, Oksana found a loving family in Zmiuoskaya's daughter and son-in-law, skater Viktor Petrenko, who became a big brother to her.

Oksana's career took off. At 15, she won the figure skating world title. The next year, 1994, she skated at the Winter Olympics at Lillehammer, Norway, and won the gold.

But her career spun out of control after Lillehammer. She moved to the United States with her coach and then bought a large house in Connecticut. As she blossomed into a full-grown teenager, her changing body made her jumps more difficult. Injuries to her knee and back kept her off the ice. Then in January 1996, she was injured in a car accident and charged with drunken and reckless driving.

Asking her many fans for understanding, Oksana is trying to turn her life around. "I really didn't understand what happened with me at that time," she has said about her Olympic victory. "I was a kid. I was scared. I was working hard. I skated. I did the best that I can do, and that's it. But after that, I'm a teenager, I'm a kid. I want to have fun. I wanted to experience life."

Her many friends and fans hope that the experiences she has had—both good and bad—will help Oksana return to the ice as a more mature and wiser person.

Opposite: *Winner of the Olympic gold medal for women's figure skating in Lillehammer, Norway, in 1994, Oksana Baiul has since faced many problems in her private and public life.*
(Reuters/Corbis-Bettmann)

boxed biography) and gymnasts *Lelia Podkopaayeva* [LEE-lee-ia Pod-Koh-PAH-ye-vah] and *Tatiana Gutsu* [Tah-TIA-nah GOOT-soo].

When Ukrainians aren't cheering on their Olympic hopefuls, they are avidly watching soccer, the nation's number one spectator sport. The best Ukrainian team and former world champion is the Dynamo team from Kyiv. Other popular competitive sports include volleyball, tennis, ice hockey, fencing, and motorcycle racing.

Among board games, none are as popular as chess, which has been played by Ukrainians for more than a thousand years. Pigeon-raising is another favorite pastime, along with gardening and the building of folk music instruments such as the lute-like *kobza* [KOB-zah] and the bandura, the national instrument of Ukraine.

One form of entertainment that is uniquely Slavic is the circus. Circuses can be found in every major city and are housed in beautiful permanent buildings. The Kyiv Circus even has a school where students train for several years to become clowns and other circus performers.

Food and Drink

Another favorite Ukrainian pastime is eating. Whether enjoying a meal at home or in a cozy restaurant, Ukrainians turn eating into a memorable experience that often takes hours.

Bread is the mainstay of the Ukrainian diet and it comes in a multitude of tantalizing varieties. There is a special kind of bread for every festive occasion. *Babka* [BAHB-kah] is a rich, sweet bread shaped like a woman in a dress (hence its name) and is eaten at Christmas and Easter. *Palianytsia* [Pah-lia-NIH-Sia] is ring shaped and a special treat at weddings. *Paska* [PAHS-Kah] is shaped like a cross and is eaten at Easter time.

Soups are also popular. *Borchuch* [BORSHCH], also known as borscht, is a beet-cabbage soup that is considered the national dish. Although it is also popular in Russia, Poland, and other Slavic countries, Ukrainians will tell you flatly it was first made in their country. In addition to the beets that give it its red color, borchuch can contain more than a dozen different vegetables and grains. It is served hot in the winter and cold in the summer.

Ukrainian food is highly seasoned and often pickled to preserve it through the long winter. Pickled foods include cucumbers, tomatoes, mushrooms, and even fruits such as apples.

One Ukrainian specialty that is enjoyed the world over is *kotleta po kievski* [Kot-LEH-tah poh KIH-yeevs-Kih]. It is a breaded chicken breast flattened and rolled around a seasoned stick of butter and then fried to tenderness. It is better known to non-Ukrainians as chicken Kiev.

Among beverages, tea is more popular than coffee, and vodka is the preferred alcoholic drink. It is usually drunk very cold in tiny glasses.

Vodka has been another point of contention with Russia lately. Cheap Ukrainian vodka has flooded the Russian market and hurt business for Russian distillers. In January 1996, the Russian government auctioned off import quotas for alcohol and in September of that year proposed introducing a 20 percent tax on all Ukrainian imports. This was met with sharp protest from Ukraine, which relies on Russia as its largest trading partner.

Holidays

Holidays are a time to celebrate the rich traditions of the past and forget about the troubles of the present.

A Ukrainian Christmas is unlike Christmas anywhere else. For one thing, the holiday is celebrated on January 7 instead of December 25. The Orthodox Church follows the old Julian calendar that is 13 days behind the newer Gregorian calendar.

This "Old Christmas," as it is called, begins on Christmas Eve with candles placed in the windows of each home to lead the Holy Family there. The Christmas Eve banquet has twelve meatless and milkless dishes, one for each of Christ's twelve apostles. To re-create the manger in Bethlehem where Jesus was born, hay is placed on the floor of each home and pets or farm animals are brought into the house, to the delight of the children.

Ukrainian Easter is even more festive than Christmas. It usually lasts from Easter Sunday through the following Thursday. *Pysanky* eggs are made, blessed by priests, and given as gifts. People visit friends and

Despite the swift course of recent events, Ukrainians, especially older ones, have not forgotten the past. These World War II veterans are celebrating Victory Day, May 9, when the Allied forces defeated the German Nazis who had killed 20 million people in Russia, Ukraine, and the other Soviet republics. (Sasha Bezzubov/Impact Visuals)

relatives, dress up in national folk costumes, and sing and dance at special Easter festivals.

Two more contemporary holidays that are close to the hearts of Ukrainians are International Women's Day on March 8 and Independence Day celebrated on August 24, when Ukraine proclaimed its independence from the Soviet Union in 1991.

NOTES

p. 83   "Girls now have few opportunities . . ." *New York Times,* January 11, 1998, p. A6.
p. 83   "I'm not sure I would go back . . ." *New York Times,* January 11, 1998, p. A6.
p. 85   "I really didn't understand . . ." *Connecticut Post,* January 5, 1998, p. C3.

10

The Cities

The cities of Ukraine are the cultural, social, and economic nerve centers of this nation. Each major city exudes a personality all its own, but they all share some things in common: a restless energy, a cultural richness, and a colorful past.

Glorious Kyiv

"All roads lead to Kyiv," goes an old Ukrainian saying. For both Ukrainians and Russians, this is no exaggeration. For centuries, Kyiv (population 2.6 million)[*] was as much the center of the eastern Slavic world as Rome was of the Mediterranean world. Before the rise of Kyiv, there were only wandering tribes in the region; after it, there rose a civilization that gave birth to Russia.

Today Kyiv is the capital of Ukraine, the ninth largest city in Europe, and the third largest city in the CIS; only Moscow and St. Petersburg are

---

[*] Unless noted, all population estimates are from 1994.

89

bigger. Like these two Russian cities, Kyiv has its own unique beauty. "To stroll off *Khreshchatyk* [Hre-SHCHAH-tik], the main street, past buildings painted in pastels and shaded by chestnuts," observes one writer, "is to feel an Old World softness that Moscow seldom matches."

Settled in the 600s or earlier by Slavic peoples, within two centuries Kyiv was the capital of the first Russian state. Under great men of vision such as Vladymyr the Great and Yaroslav the Wise, Kyivan Rus expanded and grew into a great commercial and cultural center.

The Mongolian invasion brought the glory to an end, reducing the city to rubble. After several centuries of Lithuanian and Polish rule, Kyiv came under Russian control again in the 1600s, but now Moscow, not Kyiv, was in command of this new empire. By 1800, the city was a far cry from its past grandeur, made up of a collection of three village-like settlements. One visitor at the time declared that "Kiev [Kyiv] hardly deserves to be called a city at all."

Yet from a population of 20,000 in 1800, Kyiv steadily grew to 70,000 by 1870, the year the railroad connected it with Moscow and Odesa on the Black Sea. This growth continued into the 20th century. World War II nearly destroyed Kyiv, but a strenuous rebuilding program after the war brought back much of its greatness. Another rebirth has been going on since independence in 1991. The signs and symbols of the Communist era were torn down. Streets and squares were renamed, statues of Communist leaders were taken down, and churches were converted from museums back into places of worship.

Once called the "golden-domed city" because of the gold-leaf-covered cupolas of its many churches, today Kyiv is once again a city of churches. There are some 400 of them, the finest being St. Sophia Cathedral. It is one of the few great works of the medieval period that escaped destruction during World War II. Named for the celebrated church in Byzantium after which it was modeled, St. Sophia was begun in the 11th century and took 700 years to complete.

The city's other great medieval landmark is the Monastery of the Caves. It consists of two subterranean systems of sandstone tunnels that contain the burial grounds of many famous Ukrainians, whose bodies have been miraculously preserved through the cool temperatures and good soil. Among the celebrated dead is the monk Nestor, Ukraine's first historian.

Much of Kyiv today is a modern, well-planned city, with broad boulevards and green parks. Most residents live in vast rows of apartment

St. Andrew's Cathedral is just one of some 400 churches in Kyiv, once called the "golden-domed city" for its many gold-domed churches. (Archive Photos)

houses that surround the city. They work in factories and plants that produce a myriad of products, from chemicals to cameras to heavy machinery.

Culturally speaking, Kyiv has numerous colleges, theaters, and a world-renowned ballet company. The Ukrainian Academy of Sciences is also located here. Among the many museums are the Historical Museum of Treasures, which houses a spectacular display of precious stones, coins, and other metalwork from every period of Ukrainian history. The Kyiv Museum of Ukrainian Decorative Folk Arts is another memorable place for visitors. Perhaps the most intriguing museum is the Kyiv Museum of Theatre, Music, and Cinema Arts. Most important 20th-century Ukrainian artists, actors, writers, and filmmakers are represented here by costumes, posters, manuscripts, and other memorabilia.

The spirit of independence has brought new life into one of Europe's oldest cities. The mother of all Russian cities is proud to be Ukraine's capital, basking in a colorful past but looking forward to a new and exciting future.

Kharkiv—The Boston of Ukraine

Kyiv is secure in its Ukrainian identity. Less so is Ukraine's second-largest city *Kharkiv* [HAHR-Keev] (population 1.6 million). It is located in the easternmost part of Ukraine in the upper Donets valley, only 25 miles (40.3 km) from the Russian border.

Kharkiv is one of the country's younger cities, founded by the Kozaks in 1656. It first served as a Kozak frontier headquarters and a fortress defense for Moscow's southern border. When many Kozaks rebelled against Russia several decades later, Kharkiv remained loyal to Russia under the Ukrainian Kozaks. Because of its allegiance to Russia, Kharkiv enjoyed more freedom than other Ukrainian cities for the next two centuries. Only near the end of the 1800s did Kharkiv return to its Ukrainian roots, becoming the vital center of several intellectual and literary movements. During this time it earned the nickname "the Boston of Ukraine." In 1919, under Soviet domination, Kharkiv become the capital of the Soviet republic of Ukraine. It remained so until 1934, when the capital was moved to Kyiv.

World War II brought disaster for Kharkiv. The Germans occupied the city for nearly two years and killed 100,000 people. The Soviets rebuilt the city, filling its streets with huge government buildings and massive squares. Kharkiv's *Dzherzhinsk* (Dzehr-ZHINSK) Square is one of the largest of its kind in the world.

Kharkiv's factories manufacture aircraft, agricultural machinery, and motorcycles. But it is the city's cultural life that is most vibrant. Kharkiv University is one of Ukraine's leading institutes for higher learning, and the Kharkiv Art Museum and History Museum hold enormous collections of great art and artifacts.

Russian is still spoken by 94 percent of the people of Kharkiv. The changing of street signs and other city signs to the Ukrainian language is steady but slow. For all its Ukrainian traditions, Kharkiv remains a city caught between two cultures.

Odesa by the Sea

If Kharkiv is Ukraine's Russian city, Odesa (population 1.1 million) is its melting pot. More than 100 nationalities call Ukraine's largest port their home, a fact in which the city takes great pride. Odesa was first settled

Chersonesos—A Treasured Past

Outside of Sevastople on the Black Sea coast lies what archaeologists are calling one of the best preserved sites of the ancient world—Chersonesos [CHER-so-NEE-sus], the northernmost colony of the early Greeks.

Chersonesos, which means "peninsula" in Greek, is more than one site. As archaeologists dig down, they have uncovered the ruins of one civilization after another.

"There is no place on earth like Chersonesos," says Dr. Joseph Coleman Carter, director of the Institute of Classical Archaeology at the University of Texas. "Greek, Roman, and Byzantine all had their day. Every epoch built its way of life on this soil. . . . If we could restore what is here and present that to people, it would be remarkable."

Unfortunately, that won't be easy. The ambitious restoration will cost millions of dollars, which Ukraine can hardly afford without outside help. Secondly, the Ukrainian Orthodox Church, which owns much of the property where the ruins are located, is opposed to its development and favors destroying the pagan buildings and artifacts.

The Ukrainian Cultural Ministry and many other Ukrainians support the Chersonesos project, but the church is a power to be reckoned with. As a result of these problems, Chersonesos has made the 100 most-endangered cultural sites' list of the World Monument Fund. While the controversy continues, Dr. Carter and other archaeologists continue to unearth the past's priceless treasures, from Scythian tombs to Greek farmhouses. "It's been here for thousands of years," says Leonid *Marchenko* [MAHR-chen-Koh], a director of a local museum. "It's all in one place. We just need to let it out."

by Ottoman Turks in 1415. It wasn't called by its present name until the Russians took it over in the 1790s. They named it after the ancient Greek colony of Odessos, which they erroneously believed was previously located there. The Russians transformed Odesa into a naval port and a fortress to defend the country from Europeans to the south. By the late 19th century, it was the largest city in the Ukraine and the second largest port in the Russian Empire after St. Petersburg. But it also became a center for new ideas, some of them opposed by the Russian government.

When the Revolution of 1905 broke out, Odesa's workers were in the forefront of the rebellion. The crew of the battleship *Potemkin* mutinied in the Black Sea and found support and shelter in Odesa. This historical moment is immortalized in the 1925 silent film classic *Potemkin*. The film's climax takes place on the Maritime Stairs, 192 steps that link a main boulevard of the city with the port section. Director Sergei Eisenstein's filming of the massacre of innocent residents on the steps by the czar's Kozaks never actually took place, but the grand staircase to the sea has been renamed the "Potemkin Steps" in honor of the mutineers.

Today Odesa remains a cosmopolitan city of beaches, spas, and multiethnic communities. "Odesa has always shown more color, spirit and irreverence than other cities of the former Soviet Union," write authors Linda Hodges and George Chumak. "There's an excitement, a verve, an anything-is-possible feeling in its streets."

Lviv—Capital of Western Ukraine

Western Ukraine has always had a different outlook from the rest of the country. Ukrainian nationalism did not have to be reintroduced in western Ukraine because it never left. Geographically the closest part of the country to the West and the last region to come under Soviet domination, western Ukraine is home to a proud and spirited people.

Lviv (population 800,000), the major city of west Ukraine, has been called the most Ukrainian of Ukrainian cities. It is located near the Polish border in the northern foothills of the Carpathian Mountains. Its turbulent history began with its founding in 1256 by Prince *Danylo Holytsky* [Dah-NIH-loh GHA-lih-tskiy] of *Galicia-Volyin* [GHA-lih-Koh-Voh-LIN], a medieval kingdom south of Poland. He named it after his son Prince *Lev*.

Over the next 500 years, this trading center and outpost was ruled in succession by the Poles, the Turks, the Swedes, and then the Poles again. In 1772, with the first partition of Poland, it came under the rule of the Austro-Hungarian Empire. Lviv became the capital of Galicia, no longer a kingdom but a region of southeastern Poland. When the empire crumbled after World War I, Lviv became the capital of the Western Ukrainian Democratic Republic. One of the shortest-living republics to emerge from the war, it was seized by the new republic of Poland in 1919. It remained part of Poland until the Soviets annexed it in 1939.

Despite German occupation, Lviv was spared the wholesale destruction of other Ukrainian cities. The Soviets could not reach the region until the war was nearly over and the Germans had already been vanquished. Western Ukraine was openly rebellious to Soviet rule from the start. Lviv was the focal point of a dissident movement in the 1980s that propelled the country toward independence.

Lviv's long past lives on in its famous Market Square, which dates back to 1380 and lies in the heart of the city's old town. You might not think of a cemetery as a tourist attraction, but Lviv's *Lychakiv* [Lih-SHAH-Keev] Cemetery is considered one of the most beautiful in Europe, with thousands of monuments and sculptures amid lush greenery. Among the famous Ukrainians buried here is writer Ivan Franko, for whom the city's Ivan Franko University is named.

Yalta—Jewel of the Crimea

Yalta [IAL-tah] (population 89,000, 1991 estimate), located in southern Crimea on the Black Sea, will forever be connected with the meeting of the "Big Three" Allied leaders of World War II: Prime Minister Winston Churchill of England, President Franklin Roosevelt of the United States, and Soviet leader Joseph Stalin. They met here at *Livadia* [Lee-VAH-dee-ya], summer estate of Czar Nicholas II, in February 1945 to plan the postwar peace, a peace that was destroyed by Stalin's plan to dominate Eastern Europe.

But Yalta had a long and colorful history well before the Yalta Conference. It was founded as a Greek colony, Yalita, in the first century A.D. and was passed back and forth among invaders and conquerors for centuries. In 1783, the Russians moved in when they annexed all of Crimea from Turkey. Forty years later, a Russian prince named *Vorontsove* [Voh-rohn-TSOH-veh] turned the modest town into a small city.

Yalta's Mediterranean climate and beautiful beaches attracted Russia's nobility, who built summer estates there for their families. During the Soviet era, Communist leaders built handsome dachas, Russian country

This ornate building is part of Livadia, the summer palace of Czar Nicholas II. It was here in this idyllic setting that Churchill, Roosevelt, and Stalin met in February 1945 for the famous Yalta Conference. (Underwood & Underwood/ Corbis-Bettmann)

homes, in or near Yalta. Nikita Khrushchev's dacha, later taken over by his successor, Leonid Brezhnev, was equipped with a 250-foot-deep (76.2 m) bomb shelter.

Writers have also been attracted to Yalta's natural beauty. Playwright and short-story writer Anton Chekhov spent his last years here, writing the plays *The Cherry Orchard* and *Three Sisters*. Today his home is a museum. There is also a theater named in Chekhov's honor.

Besides tourism, Yalta's major industries are wine making and tobacco processing.

Three Industrial Giants

North of the Crimea in southeastern Ukraine lie three cities that are among the nation's industrial giants.

Dnepropetrovsk [Dneep-ROH-pet-ROV-skeh] (population 1.2 million, 1989 estimate), located on the mighty Dnipro River, is in the heart of the coal-mining region known as Donbas and is the center of Ukraine's steel and iron industry. It is also one of the country's major river ports. For all its industry, Dnepropetrovsk has more than 3,000 acres (1,215 ha) of parks for its citizens to enjoy.

The city was founded in 1787 by Russian general Grigori Potemkin who named it *Ekaterinoslav* [Ye-Kah-teh-rih-nos-LAHV], after his queen, Catherine the Great. It was given its current name in 1926.

A little to the south of Dnepropetrovsk, on the opposite bank of the Dnipro, sits *Zaporizhzhya* [Zah-poh-REEZH-zhya] (population 897,000, 1989 est.), site of the *Dneproges* [Dneep-ROH-GES] hydroelectric dam and power station, one of the first and largest of its kind in the former Soviet Union. The name means beyond the rapids. For three centuries, it was the headquarters of the Zaporizhzhya Kozaks in their struggle against the Poles.

The dam, rebuilt after World War II, is the city's blessing and its curse. The waste from the dam and nearby plants has seriously polluted Zaporizhzhya and the surrounding area.

Pollution has been better controlled in *Donetsk* [Doh-NYETSK] (population 1.1 million) farther east on the Kalmius River. Surrounded by coal mines and steel mills, Donetsk has more park land than any other Ukrainian city. Despite its industrial reputation, it also has a rich cultural life and is home to five colleges and universities, the Ukrainian Theatre of Music and Drama, and a popular puppet theater.

Industry and culture, modernity and tradition, the great cities of Ukraine have been able to balance the needs of the larger nation with the needs of the people who live and work there.

NOTES

p. 90   "To stroll off Khreshchatyk . . ." Edwards, "Ukraine: Running on Empty," p. 44.

p. 90   "Kiev hardly deserves to be called . . ." Michael F. Hamm, *Kiev: A Portrait, 1800–1917* (Princeton, N.J.: Princeton University Press, 1993), p. 21.

p. 93   "There is no place on earth . . ." *New York Times,* November 25, 1997, p. F1.

p. 93   "It's been here for thousands of years . . ." *New York Times,* p. F8.

p. 94   "Odesa has always shown . . ." Hodges and Chumak, p. 289.

11

Present Problems and Future Solutions

*E*ver since the glory days of Kyivan Rus, Ukraine has been, as its name suggests, a borderland. Like other borderlands, its history has been filled with romantic outlaws, fierce invaders, and powerful conquerors. It has often found itself in a no-man's-land—neither a republic nor a colony, neither a rich land nor a poor one, not a free nation, but refusing to be an enslaved one.

Although it has been independent since 1991, Ukraine is still dependent on others for many things: energy, capital, and trade. As it enters the 21st century, Ukraine faces many problems, some of them of its own devising. These problems are soluble, but working out the solutions will not be easy. It will take as much energy, imagination, and perseverance to solve them as it did to break away from the Soviet Union.

Here are six of these problems and some possible solutions.

The Soviet Factor

"It seems very strange that Ukraine . . . ever chose to become independent from us," a Russian high school teacher told an American journalist. "In the end, they won't be able to live without Russia and they'll rejoin."

Many Russians, a number of them who live in Ukraine, share this sentiment. They see Ukraine's assertion of independence as a "temporary phenomenon," something that will pass, like a fever. After all, Ukraine had been a part of the Russian and Soviet empires for more than 300 years.

Most Ukrainians view the situation differently. For them, Russia is just another of the interlopers who have taken their freedom away and drained their land of its rich resources for their own use. Ukraine has as little interest in rejoining Russia as does any other former Soviet republic.

Yet Ukraine still needs Russia at least as much as Russia needs it. Russia provides Ukraine with gas and oil—two natural resources of which this resource-rich country has little. Russia is still Ukraine's number one trade partner and is likely to remain so for some time. Ukrainian farmers regularly bring their produce to Russian markets to sell, knowing they'll get a better price for their goods there than at home.

Even if the day comes when Ukraine can stand economically independent of Russia, it will still have to deal politically with its nearest neighbor. As one Ukrainian puts it, "Russia is a huge power and it will always be next to us."

Ukraine and Russia are beginning to learn to respect each other, as the friendship treaty signed by its leaders in June 1997 proves. But treaties are one thing, and what people feel in their hearts and minds is another matter. It will take time and understanding for these two giants to work out their differences and achieve a relationship that is mutually satisfactory.

The Crimean Question

Nowhere are the tensions between Russia and Ukraine more apparent than in the Crimea. This peninsula of land extending south from Ukraine into the Black Sea wants to be independent. But Ukrainians insist the Crimea belongs to them and has since Nikita Khrushchev first gave it over to them in 1954. Ukraine is afraid that if Crimea becomes autonomous it will once again become part of Russia. Many Russians would like to see this happen, and so would many Crimeans: 70 percent of the population is Russian.

"People think they were better off before," says a Ukrainian naval captain in the Crimea, referring back to the Soviet era. "They don't remember the bad things."

One of the "bad things" that happened here under Soviet rule was the exile of the Crimea's native people, the Tatars. Stalin sent them to Siberia after World War II for supposedly collaborating with the Nazis. In the late 1980s, many of them began returning under the liberal policies of Soviet leader Mikhail Gorbachev. Today, there are some 200,000 Tatars in the Crimea.

The most contested issue in the Crimea has been the powerful Black Sea fleet in Sevastopol, Crimea's capital. The Russians said the fleet and the city are their property. Ukraine responded that the fleet was on their sovereign territory and refused to give it up. They felt that if Russia took

A Russian and a Ukrainian sailor arm wrestle at Sevastopol on the Black Sea. The contest is a friendly one but is symbolic of a larger struggle between the Ukrainians and Russians for control of the Black Sea fleet. While this contest has been resolved, tensions between the two countries continue. (Reuters/ Corbis-Bettmann)

over the fleet they would use it as a stepping stone to take over the entire region.

In the 1997 treaty between the two countries, an agreement seemed to have been reached on the Crimea (see chapter 4). But how long the agreement will last is uncertain. Ukraine's shifting relationship with Russia is still unstable, and it will certainly be affected by its developing relationship with the West.

National Security

Ukraine sees membership in NATO as a way of both asserting its independence from Russia and securing itself from outside aggression. In 1994, it joined NATO's partnership for peace program, a kind of testing ground for nations who eventually want to become full NATO members.

Poland, Hungary, and the Czech Republic are the first countries from Eastern Europe to be invited to become NATO members before the organization's 50th anniversary in 1999, but Ukraine is on the list of future invitees. In July 1997, during a NATO summit meeting in Madrid, Spain, Ukraine signed a broad charter with the organization. According to Deputy Foreign Minister *Kostyantin Gryshchenko* [Kos-tian-TIN GRIH-Shchen-Koh], the charter "clearly states the nature of our distinctive special relationship with the United States. For us, it was significant to establish that we would not find ourselves in some 'gray zone' between NATO and Russia. . . ."

While Russia has resolved many of its differences with the West and has itself joined in the NATO process, one wonders how happy it will be to see its nearest neighbor become a part of an organization that for decades it viewed as the enemy.

Crime and Corruption

On March 1997, thieves stole two famous paintings worth $800,000 from the Fine Arts Museum in *Poltava* [Pol-TAH-vah] in eastern Ukraine. This crime would not be so unusual, except that the theft occurred in broad daylight while the museum was open. Horrified patrons stood by as armed masked gunmen made off with the works of arts.

Such bold crimes have become all too commonplace in Ukraine, as they have throughout the new republics of Eastern Europe. In the wake of communism, organized crime has moved in to fill a power vacuum in many a floundering country. Some of the crime mobs operate out of Moscow and others out of Kyiv. They are involved in every kind of illegal activity, from prostitution to the smuggling of drugs and other contraband. Smuggling contraband has become a way of life for some people in western Ukraine, geographically well situated for goods passing from the West into Eastern Europe.

Other crimes, such as murder, are up, too. In April 1996, a 37-year-old accused serial killer, nicknamed "The Terminator," was arrested and charged with the murders of 52 people.

Ukraine's government has attempted to deal harshly with criminals and strictly enforces its death penalty. According to Amnesty International, more executions took place in Ukraine in 1996—167 of them—than in any other country except China.

But law and order has done little to end the rampant corruption in business and government. Bribing officials for government contracts or licenses is an everyday occurrence. As the wife of one venal businessman puts it, "anything can be done if you have money and the right connections."

One of the best connected businessmen in the Ukraine today is *Vadim Rabinovitch* [Vah-DIM Rah-bee-NOH-Vich], owner of a Ukrainian television station and the developer of the country's first five-star hotel. Rabinovitch served a long prison sentence in the Soviet Union for theft back in the 1980s. "In America," he boasts, "people get awards for what the Soviets convicted me of—successfully running a business."

But Rabinovitch's shady dealings in the more recent past have caused serious problems for his American partner, Ronald Lauder, of the Estée Lauder cosmetic empire. Lauder was shocked to learn of his partner's criminal record and has since been named in a $750-million lawsuit filed by a rival broadcaster. The rival accused their company of using "corrupt methods" to obtain a national broadcasting license and getting his revoked. Lauder pleaded innocent, and his only crime may have been not checking into Rabinovitch's background before joining forces with him. It is such entanglements that have made American businesses wary of entering the Ukrainian marketplace.

President Kuchma has pledged to clean up the corruption, but many feel it is so pervasive that it will take a much greater effort than has so far been made. Kuchma, they say, while above reproach, will have to get rid of many of the people in his government who are wheeling and dealing with private industry.

Health

The national health of Ukraine is considerably better than most of its neighbors, including Russia. The Ukrainians have been in the forefront of medical technology, and the statistics support this. The mortality rate is 22 per 1,000 births, one of the lowest among former Soviet republics. Life expectancy is 71 years, again above average for the region.

But despite these encouraging signs, there are problems in health care. The poor economy has caused serious shortages of medical supplies, especially in rural hospitals and clinics. As many as 40 percent of hospitals reuse hypodermic needles and have no hot water. Lack of sewage connections in the countryside has helped the spread of disease. In September 1994, an outbreak of cholera in the south claimed 17 lives. Shortages of vaccines have resulted in outbreaks of diphtheria.

Public health must become a top priority for the government if future epidemics are to be prevented.

The Environment

The specter of the Chornobyl nuclear disaster hangs heavily over the Ukrainian landscape (see boxed feature). What happened there in 1986 has made Ukrainians painfully aware of the environment and the importance of protecting it. But in 1998, the nuclear station remained open. The government is holding it hostage from the international community until more than a billion dollars promised in funding for two new atomic power stations is given.

The ongoing legacy of Chornobyl is a grim one, but there are other equally serious threats to Ukraine's environment that are preventable. Two of the

The Curse of Chornobyl

It had been 10 years since that terrible early morning of April 26, 1986, when Reactor No. 4 at the Chornobyl nuclear plant exploded. But for the thousands of Ukrainians who gathered in silence at a tribute service in the town of *Slavutych* [Slah-VOO-tich], it was a curse they still lived with. Since the explosion, some 4,300 people had died as a direct result of the accident and exposure to high doses of radiation. Thousands more children, born after the accident, were affected in their mothers' wombs and suffer from various forms of cancer, respiratory ailments, and a host of other diseases related to radiation exposure. Every year, many of these children travel to the United States, Canada, and other countries where they are treated for their health problems by compassionate doctors and hospitals, often free of charge.

Chornobyl itself is a ghost town, as are 75 villages that surround it. Other villages in the area, like *Maryaniska* [Mah-RYA-nee-Sha], are supposedly safe to live in, but many people question their safety amid nuclear contamination.

"Only six feet from the [contamination] sign it's supposedly all right to have a garden," says one local woman. "I don't know what to believe. Nobody tells us the truth. Everything is contaminated in the whole area, but they tell us everything is fine."

Ironically, many of the people at the tribute service still work at Chornobyl's three remaining reactors. Although the possibility of another meltdown is all too real, Ukraine has continued to take the risk to get the nuclear energy this energy-poor nation needs so desperately. Hopefully, after many delays, the final closing of Chornobyl will take place soon.

At the 1997 tribute service, President Kuchma said that "the nuclear burden on the planet has to be reduced." The sad truth is if Ukraine never has another nuclear accident, the curse of Chornobyl will continue to plague its children and their children's children for many years to come. Let us hope that the Ukrainians, and all of us, have learned something from this bitter lesson.

country's major rivers, the Don and the Dnipro, are full of sewage and industrial waste, spreading their pollutants throughout the countryside.

In even worse condition is the Black Sea, where pollution is so bad that 20 out of 26 species of fish found there have completely died out

This abandoned amusement park in the city of Pripyat is an eerie reminder of the havoc wreaked by the nuclear accident at Chornobyl in 1987. Some 75 villages surrounding Chornobyl have been abandoned as uninhabitable since the accident. Note the deserted high-rise apartment buildings in the background. (Gleb Kosowkov/Impact Visuals)

over the past 30 years due to a lack of oxygen and light. Instead, the sea is a breeding ground for jellyfish that thrive on fish larvae and phytoplankton that live on human waste.

A task force of environmentalists from Ukraine and five other countries that border the body of water are working tirelessly to save the Black Sea. They signed an agreement in the fall of 1996 to set up regulations for commercial fishing, shipping, and development of the coast.

"If the habitats of these species can be protected and further damage avoided," says marine environmentalist Dr. Laurence Mee, "the sea may slowly recover from the bottom up . . . if we act now."

Ukraine, with its rich natural resources, thousand-year-old culture, and resilient, optimistic people, has the potential to be one of the major nations of Europe. It has much to overcome, but it also has much to gain. Only by facing its problems fearlessly will it fulfill that potential.

NOTES

p. 100   "It seems very strange . . ." *Washington Post,* January 5, 1997, p. A17. CD NewsBank.

p. 100   "Russia is a huge power . . ." *Washington Post,* January 5, 1997, p. A17. CD NewsBank.

p. 101   "People think they were better off . . ." Peter T. White, "Crimea: Pearl of a Fallen Empire," *National Geographic,* September 1994, p. 109.

p. 102   "clearly states the nature . . ." *Washington Times,* July 23, 1997, CD NewsBank.

p. 103   "anything can be done . . ." White, p. 104.

p. 103   "In America, people get awards . . . *Wall Street Journal,* September 12, 1997, A18.

p. 105   "Only six feet from the [contamination] sign . . ." Edwards, "Ukraine: Running on Empty," p. 47.

p. 105   "the nuclear burden on the planet . . ." *Facts On File: World News Digest,* May 9, 1996, p. 327.

p. 106   "If the habitats of these species . . ." *Christian Science Monitor,* December 13, 1996, p. 6. CD NewsBank.

Chronology

c. 4000 B.C.	The Trypillians settle in present-day Ukraine and establish first communities.
c. 1000 B.C.	Nomadic warrior tribes, including the Cimmerians, migrate into area.
c. 700 B.C.	The Scythians invade Ukraine and control it for 500 years.
c. A.D. 300	The Varangians, or Rus, arrive from Scandinavia and unify the peoples under their leader, Rurik.
A.D. 987	Vladymyr the Great converts Kyivan Rus to Christianity.
978–1054	Yaroslav the Wise makes Kyiv one of the largest and most powerful cities in Europe.
1169	Kyiv, now in decline, is seized and looted by Kyiv prince Andrei Bogolyubsky, who moves the capitol to Vladymyr.
1223	The Mongols conquer Kyiv and control it for the next two centuries.
1569	The Poles take over Kyivan Rus lands, now called *Ukrainia,* meaning "borderlands."
1648–49	The Kozaks, fierce warriors, led by Bohdan Khmelnytsky, rise up against the Poles and seize Kyiv.

1654	The Kozaks and Russians sign the Treaty of Peruyaslav, uniting their countries against Poland.
1659	The Kozaks, now aligned with the Poles, defeat the Russians at the Battle of Konotip.
1666	Poland and Russia divide the Ukraine between them.
1781	Kozak power is broken with the end of the hetmanate; Russia is in full control of the Ukraine.
1825	The Decembrist Revolution against the Russian czar fails in St. Petersburg.
1905	The Revolution of 1905 fails to overthrow the czar; Odesa is attacked by the czar's Kozaks for harboring mutineers of the battleship *Potemkin*.
1917	The October Revolution overthrows the czar and sets off a civil war between Bolsheviks and anti-Bolshevik forces.
January 22, 1918	Ukraine declares its independence, becoming the Ukrainian National Republic.
1921	The new Soviet state overthrows independent Ukraine and absorbs it. Within a year, it becomes one of the first socialist republics of the Soviet Union.
1929	Soviet leader Joseph Stalin begins the collectivization of farms in Ukraine and elsewhere; millions of Ukrainians are imprisoned, executed, or forced to emigrate for resisting.
1932–33	Some seven million Ukrainians die of starvation in the worst human-made famine in recorded history.
1938	Nikita Khrushchev is appointed Communist leader in Ukraine and purges the Communist Party there in a reign of terror.
June 1941	Germany invades Ukraine in a major attack on the Soviet Union during World War II; many Ukrainians collaborate with the Nazis.
1945	The war ends in German defeat; many Ukrainians are imprisoned, exiled, or executed by the Soviets for collaborating with the Nazis.

1946	A natural famine devastates Ukraine.
1954	The Soviets turn the Crimea over to Ukraine as a goodwill gesture.
1956	Khrushchev takes over as supreme Soviet leader.
1964	Khrushchev falls from power and is replaced by Leonid Brezhnev, who is Ukrainian by birth.
1982	Brezhnev dies at age 76.
1985	Mikhail Gorbachev comes to power and loosens the Soviet grip on Ukrainian nationalism.
April 26, 1986	An explosion at a nuclear plant at Chornobyl, Ukraine, exposes 100,000 people to high levels of radiation.

1989

| September | The popular movement *Rukh* is born, calling out for political change in Ukraine. |
| November | Vladymyr Ivashko, a moderate Communist leader, comes to power. |

1991

August 19–21	An attempted coup in Moscow of Communist hard-liners fails and is seen as communism's last gasp.
August 24	The Ukrainian parliament declares independence from the Soviet Union.
December 1	A national referendum on independence passes overwhelmingly; Leonid Kravchuk is elected first president of the new republic.

1992

| October | Leonid Kuchma is appointed prime minister. |

1993

| September | Kuchma resigns in disgust from Kravchuk's corrupt government. |

1994

June	Kuchma is elected president.
August	Sevastopol in the Crimea declares itself a Russian city.
October–November	Kuchma visits the United States and Canada, seeking financial aid for Ukraine.

1995

March	The Ukrainian government ends a potential rebellion in the Crimea.

1996

June	A new constitution increasing the powers of the president is approved.

1997

May	Russian leader Boris Yeltsin makes his first trip to Ukraine and signs a friendship treaty with President Kuchma.
July	Ukraine signs a charter with NATO at a summit meeting in Madrid, paving the way for eventual membership in the organization.
August	Ukraine celebrates its sixth anniversary of independence with military exercises that include American sailors and marines.

1998

April	The Ukraine Communist Party wins one-quarter of the vote in national elections.
August	State Statistics Committee reports in July that country experienced deflation for first time since independence, with a 2.3 percent reduction in food prices; President Kuchma celebrates his 60th birthday in the Crimea with representatives and leaders of Eastern Europe and the United States.

Further Reading

Nonfiction Books

Gosnell, Kelvin. *Belarus, Ukraine, and Moldova* (Brookfield, Conn.: Millbrook Press, 1992.) A general introduction to Ukraine and two other former Soviet republics for middle grade readers.

Hodges, Linda, and Chumak, George. *Hippocrene Language and Travel Guide to Ukraine* (New York: Hippocrene Books, 1994.) Although a travel guide, this book is an excellent and concise introduction to the country and its people with up-to-date information.

Lerner Publishers. *Ukraine Then and Now* (Minneapolis, Minn.: Lerner Publications, 1993.) Another general introduction for middle grades, nicely designed with good pictures.

Oparenko, Christina. *The Ukraine* (New York: Chelsea House, 1988.) Largely outdated book for young adults that deals more with Ukrainian culture and history than contemporary issues.

Resnick, Abraham. *The Commonwealth of Independent States: Russia and the Other Republics* (Chicago: Children's Press, 1994.) Another in the Enchantment of the World series. Material on Ukraine is sketchy.

Fiction and Plays

Chekhov, Anton. *Four Great Plays* (New York: Bantam, 1963, paper.) The finest works of the greatest of Russian/Ukrainian playwrights. *The Cherry Orchard* and *Three Sisters* were written in the Crimea.

Gogol Nikolai. *Taras Bulba: A Tale of the Cossacks* (New York: Knopf, 1931.) Tragic but rousing novel of fictional Kozak leader by a great Ukrainian writer, who wrote in Russian.

Index

Entries are filed letter by letter. **Boldface** page numbers indicate main discussion of topic; *italic* numbers indicate illustrations; page numbers followed by *c* indicate chronology; those followed by *m* indicate maps.